METAPHOR AND MEANING IN D. H. LAWRENCE'S LATER NOVELS

METAPHOR AND MEANING IN
D. H. LAWRENCE'S
LATER NOVELS

JOHN B. HUMMA

University of Missouri Press
Columbia and London

5   4   3   2   1   94   93   92   91   90

Library of Congress Cataloging-in-Publication Data

Humma, John B., 1940–
     Metaphor and meaning in D.H. Lawrence's later novels / John B.
     Humma.
          p.   cm.
     Includes bibliographical references.
     ISBN 0-8262-0742-1 (alk. paper)
     1. Lawrence, D. H. (David Herbert), 1885–1930—Criticism and
interpretation.   2. Myth in literature.   3. Metaphor.   I. Title.
PR6023.A93Z631923   1990
823′.912—dc20   90-32579
                                                                      CIP

∞™ This paper meets the minimum requirements of
the American National Standard for Permanence of Paper
for Printed Library Materials, Z39.48, 1984.

Designer: Kristie Lee
Typesetter: Connell-Zeko Type & Graphics
Printer: Thomson-Shore, Inc.
Binder: Thomson-Shore, Inc.
Typeface: Cheltenham Light

*For Susan, Lari, Julie, Lizzie,
James, and Berchie*

Contents

Lawrence's later fiction offers a different sort of challenge than that of the middle (the "great") fiction. Though it appears looser, more offhand as it were, it has its own demands to make on the reader. These demands—and the attendant rewards—are the subject of this book.

The word *meaning* in the title needs amplification. I am interested chiefly in the way that Lawrence's art contributes to the meanings of the later novels. The particular aspect of Lawrence's art that concerns me most is the use to which he puts metaphor. Meaning by itself is outside the realm of this study. Meaning as it is reinforced by and achieved through metaphor is, however, this book's center. Though it would be sheer silliness to claim that one cannot get the "idea" of these novels without the benefit of this study, I would say that understanding what Lawrence attempts through his often elaborate textures of metaphor enriches our appreciation of them. Meaning by itself is threadbare, a paraphrase on the page, a summary or pronouncement merely. The vitality of Lawrence's fiction is in his language and in his characters, who themselves, of course, are borne up by the language.

I have analyzed these later fictions always with the view that to realize fully the ideas in them we have to appreciate the strategies that Lawrence is working with language. In one sense it is obvious that meaning relies entirely on language. What may not be so obvious, since it is often over-looked, is the extent to which the morality of literature is embedded in the coherence of the language. This is another way of saying that art and morality, in fiction at least, cannot be separated. My purpose has been nei-ther more nor less than to show *how*, in these longer fictions of Lawrence, this is so, and to claim for them a due that, largely, we have not paid them.

If the novel is the great book of life, as I agree with Lawrence that it is, then the engagement with language is an engagement with life itself, and the discoveries we make or find in language are discoveries in our lives as well—never of "meanings" in any abstract sense, since discovery is about what things *are*, not what they mean. Lawrence's works often confuse read-ers because Lawrence himself does not always know what his discoveries mean. His novels, indeed, often have their own built-in indeterminacies: the critic does not have to worry the text to locate them.

Many others have gone before me in treating the later novels. I have benefited from their studies, often excellent, of individual works, a number of which I have had occasion to refer to. None of these studies, however, has looked at the language of Lawrence's longer fictions as this one does, finding, as it were, a linguistic distinctiveness (and coherence) in them as a body. Donald Gutierrez has written about several of the later works in his *Lapsing Out: Embodiments of Death and Rebirth in the Last Writings of D. H. Lawrence*, but his focus, of course, is thematic. Lydia Blanchard has also written impressively about Lawrence's language in various of the novels, earlier as well as later, but she has her own concerns, which are different from mine. Of an earlier generation of critics, I have been influenced both by F. R. Leavis and Eliseo Vivas. Leavis was the first to establish firmly the artistic merits of a number of the later writings. Vivas also directed our attention to the art of the novels, and though I think he is largely wrong in his assessments of the later works, he is so, for me at least, in a provocative and stimulating way. And Harry T. Moore, of course, under whom I studied at Southern Illinois, by the sheer force of his personal presence in the Lawrence field, has caused us to view almost everything Lawrence wrote with interest.

I have found that undergraduate students, and many graduate students as well, respond to Lawrence better if I use one of the later works rather than *Sons and Lovers* (or *The Rainbow* or *Women in Love*, though I seldom initiate students to Lawrence with either of these). The reason for this, in part, is that these works are shorter, feel lighter—to the eye as well as the hand. But what these particular readers chiefly respond to is the liveliness of the later fictions, or their "quickness," as Lawrence would say. They have not, on first reading, thought very much about metaphor or noticed very much about it. But when I begin to draw out some of Lawrence's strategies with language, they nearly always come to express an even greater appreciation of these works. This study, in great measure, is the result of my own appreciation of them.

Acknowledgments

I am indebted to the National Endowment for the Humanities for two Summer Seminar fellowships that enabled me to study first under Andrew Wright and then under Ralph Rader. From them and from my colleagues in these seminars, I gained immeasurably.

I am indebted to the Department of English and Philosophy at Georgia Southern University and to the administration of the college for grants and released time to pursue research and writing. To my colleagues in the department, I owe thanks for not letting the demands of their teaching loads, committee activities, and their own work (what there is time for) drain them of the intellectual vitality from which I have so often taken nourishment.

I owe thanks to James C. Cowan and Keith Sagar, whose perceptive comments on the manuscript have saved me several embarrassments and helped to make the study a good deal stronger.

I must thank James Benziger, my dissertation director quite a few years ago, who encouraged me initially in a paper I wrote comparing Blake and Lawrence for his English Romanticism course and who, more than any teacher I had, took the pains (often with injury, I am afraid, to his patience) to improve my writing.

Finally, I am grateful to my wife Susan, whose scrupulous proofreading had to be an act of love. Her companionship has made the whole thing easier.

I have used the Cambridge edition, when possible, for Lawrence's works. For full information about the texts, see the Bibliography. Permission has been granted to quote from the following:

Aaron's Rod. Copyright © 1988 by the Estate of Mrs. Frieda Lawrence Ravagli. Excerpts reprinted by permission of Laurence Pollinger Ltd.

The Escaped Cock. Copyright © 1973 by the Estate of Mrs. Frieda Lawrence Ravagli. Excerpts reprinted by permission of Laurence Pollinger Ltd.

Kangaroo. Copyright © 1951 by Frieda Lawrence. Excerpts reprinted by permission of Viking Penguin, Inc.

"The Ladybird," in *Four Short Novels.* Copyright © 1951 by Frieda Lawrence. Excerpts reprinted by permission of Viking Penguin, Inc.

The Plumed Serpent. Copyright © 1987 by the Estate of Mrs. Frieda Lawrence Ravagli. Excerpts reprinted by permission of Laurence Pollinger Ltd.

Four chapters of this study have previously appeared in journals in slightly different form. I wish to thank the following for allowing me to use these materials in this book: *The D. H. Lawrence Review*, where the chapters on *The Plumed Serpent* and *The Ladybird* first appeared; *PMLA*, where the chapter on *Lady Chatterley's Lover* first appeared; and *South Atlantic Review*, where the chapter on *Kangaroo* first appeared.

METAPHOR AND MEANING IN D. H. LAWRENCE'S LATER NOVELS

Chapter 1

Introduction
Myth and Metaphor in Lawrence

Mythology is central in Lawrence's fiction. A good deal has been written about its configurations in the novels and stories, especially in the later ones, with their Pans, Dionysuses, and Quetzalcoatls. As these names suggest, Lawrence, unlike Blake, did not create a personal mythology; but like Blake and Nietzsche, his was a mythology of integration, of organicism. I prefer the word *myth*, with its larger, profounder implications of sustaining fictions—the fictions that finally are truths.

Lawrence's great novels, without question, are *The Rainbow* and *Women in Love*. They are great because, beyond the particular mythologies—Norse, Greek, biblical—that help to consolidate meaning, they somehow become the myths. We can shake the specific mythologies out of them, and they retain their imposing mythic dimensions.

The later novels, those written in Lawrence's last decade, are lesser almost in proportion to the extent that the imported mythologies can be shook out of them. The work that has the greatest freight of mythology, for instance, is *The Plumed Serpent*, and it is Lawrence's most conspicuous failure. The majority of the other late novels and novellas, however, are small but wonderful successes containing the substrative (as it must be) element of myth that is among their chief appeals.

Myth in the sense that I am speaking of it is symbolic in presentation and in consequence. Thus, early in *Lady Chatterley's Lover*, we encounter Mellors, gun in hand, advancing with "swift menace" upon Connie and Sir Clifford. I had never thought much about this particular scene until recently when, rereading the novel before teaching it once more, I was struck by this passage's peculiar forcefulness. Looking more closely at the way Lawrence managed the episode and at his orchestration of the imagery, I began to appreciate just how rich the symbolic dimension of this encounter was: Mellors as a "green man," something out of the past, the deep woods, is a profoundly mythic figure, an archetype, a threat to the shallow well-being of the present age. Just as he is a menace to both lord and lady, so too is the book—through its first three-quarters anyway—a threat to the reader. I then examined more closely both the action of the novel and the imagery. I began to see how in this book Lawrence has worked his language skillfully and patiently in service of his ideas: it is the

1

texture of interlocking or interpenetrating metaphors that both reinforces and creates the action and that produces the book's powerful mythic aspect. Way leading on to way, I began to see that the other later novels and novellas also achieved their particular effects through a very careful articulation of the language. When I compared the language, for instance, of the novels after *Aaron's Rod* with that in the novels before it, I observed that Lawrence did not start writing in this metaphorical mode until *Aaron's Rod*—a circumstance that is the subject of my second chapter.

This study, then, explores the language—and the mythic dimensions served by it—in the longer fiction of Lawrence's last decade, focusing specifically on the language and myth in those works written from the time of the final drafting of *Aaron's Rod*. In these works, Lawrence develops a sense of craft (as opposed to a sense of style, which he owned in abundance) that he usually is given little credit for having. Thus, the craft that we see emerging in the later novels differs categorically from that of the earlier fiction. I speak of craft, at any rate, according to our understanding of its being usually, but not necessarily, a good thing: perhaps the price he paid for it was the failure to produce another work on the great, imaginative order of *Women in Love*. I prefer to think, however, that the craft of these later works is compensatory for the loss of power that produced the undisputed masterpieces. Despite our general unwillingness to recognize it, these later works have the sort of architectonics, the sense of texture and form, that the "new critic" in us appreciates, perhaps even without thinking to look for it or expecting to find it. Lawrence's "technique" in these novels, the way he works with language, is what is most important about them as literature or art. To be sure, none of them are flawless; several have prominent structural deficiencies. In spite of these (sometimes only apparent) problems, however, they evidence a maturity, a new awareness about metaphorical texture, that makes the characterization of them as a "falling off" misleading and unfair. They may not be great in the way that the Brangwen novels are, but they embody nonetheless an important advance of another kind.

Though critics in recent years have paid the novels from *Aaron's Rod* through *The Escaped Cock* somewhat more respect than they received in former times, these works, as I am considering them here, remain relatively underexposed. To be sure, *The Plumed Serpent* and *Lady Chatterley's Lover* are hardly neglected—certainly not the latter. The others have benefited from some excellent considerations, including, to name a few, those of James C. Cowan, John Worthen, Keith Sagar, Daniel J. Schneider, Michael Squires, Dennis Jackson, L. D. Clark, and Julian Moynahan. Yet, though technique figures in most of these considerations, it nearly always is subordinated to theme or ideology. My effort here has been to approach

Lawrence's meanings through his language, to show how he works toward and through his ethic by a process of discovery involving imagery and mythology that is advanced by language at almost every turn.

In one sense, it may seem fantastic to suggest that these later works, in which polemic often appears extravagant, in which summary so frequently appears to dwarf scene—it may seem fantastic to suggest that these works, on balance, evidence anything approaching what Mark Schorer calls "technique as discovery." After all, Schorer was extremely critical of so fine a work as *Sons and Lovers* largely for its failure to discover its meanings through technique. In another sense, however, in the later fictions beginning with *Aaron's Rod* (the portion composed later) and *The Ladybird*,[1] it is precisely discovery that is taking place when Lawrence's metaphors function to *enable* the meanings. In these works, metaphor becomes inseparable from action and from meaning. The imagery of *Sons and Lovers*, to a lesser extent, and that of *The Rainbow* and *Women in Love*, to a much greater extent, is predominately *symbolic*. But the fiction of the 1920s works chiefly through metaphor or, as in the instance of *Kangaroo*, uses not so much symbol as symbolic details that function in much the same way as the metaphors in the later novels—that is, as a means to discovery, in the sense of Lawrence's working toward his own understanding, and as an enabling of discovery, in the sense of the reader's understanding. When the imagery fails to enable meaning, as in *The Plumed Serpent*, it fails in good measure because the meaning itself does not hold up: it is hollow or pernicious. The success or failure of Lawrence's imagery becomes, interestingly, a gauge of the soundness of the ideas in the book.

The study of Lawrence's later fiction has become a discovery for me in still another way. As his technique in these works became clearer, I began to see more plainly how they were generically different from all the work preceding them—not just the three great novels, but also those novels and the novellas in between: *The Lost Girl*, much of *Aaron's Rod*, *The Fox*, *The Captain's Doll*. If one did not know from the letters that *The Ladybird*, published originally with *The Fox* and *The Captain's Doll*, was written after them, one could prove it textually on the basis of the way that this novella uses metaphor. Before *The Ladybird* Lawrence was essentially a user of symbols: the shattered ball and the Christmas tree are symbols in *Aaron's Rod*; the fox and the glacier are symbols in the companion novels. But the symbolic properties of the scarab in *The Ladybird*, as I shall show, become absorbed within Lawrence's extended metaphor there, as in the latter part of *Aaron's Rod* the rod becomes absorbed in a complex of meta-

---

1. I have italicized all titles of Lawrence's short novels whether they were published separately or not.

phorical imagery. It is thus that *Aaron's Rod* is transitional. The first part, written as early as 1917, uses its images as symbols; the latter part, that written in 1921, finds Lawrence, in his weaving of metaphor, moving toward his final method. Excluding *The Virgin and the Gipsy* (written probably in 1925 but not published in Lawrence's lifetime), all of his longer fiction written after *Aaron's Rod* is intrinsically different from the longer fiction that preceded it.

This book, then, is a study of Lawrence's "art"—I use the word in its broadest sense—in the later novels and, as such, is a reassessment of them. I want to show that these works have much more going for them than they are customarily allowed. They display a demanding intricacy, an intricacy establishing the complexity of argument and action. Though a book like Eliseo Vivas's *The Failure and the Triumph of Art* is almost thirty years behind us, the vigor of Vivas's criticism of most of the later fiction (the "failures") still has the power to persuade. But what Vivas misses, as do a number of critics after him, is a whole dimension of the art, a dimension that is not only rich and interesting in its own right, but one that helps to organize all the rest. The imagery is frequently unnoticed because it functions so often as a sort of under-meaning. But in Lawrence, where so often blood-consciousness (what goes on *inside, under*) is what matters really, to miss the undergirding metaphors is to miss an organic element of no mean significance. This imagery is not just local, external, outside—so much ornamentation; but extended, connective, interpenetrating—central and vital and informing of the rest. To miss it is perhaps to miss everything.

Why it is missed is not hard to figure out. Lawrence is doing other things simultaneously, and we do not read much for description anymore. Moreover, readers of Lawrence are too frequently (I speak for myself also) hounds on the scent of his ideas. Whether we are disposed to like what he is saying or not (I find plenty to disagree with), he is seldom uninteresting. The exception to this statement, for me at least, is *The Plumed Serpent*. What does interest me though is why this novel goes wrong, and as I suggested earlier, if we wish to look for the reasons for the triumph or the failure of the art of the later fiction, we must look first at the imagery.

We may read a writer at first for what he says but we continue to read him, *if* we continue to read him, for how he says it. Thus I have no central thesis to advance about the Lawrencian ethos, but I believe that to find it, find it surely, we will best do so in the imagery. The imagery does not lie: it reveals the hollowness of the ideas in a book like *The Plumed Serpent*. Moreover, while the imagery in Lawrence's later fiction is mulled, considered, deliberative, and thus marked by craft, the same imagery is also the intuitive, organic component of the action and the ideas—hence, the art. It is, to use Eliseo Vivas's term, "constitutive."[2]

As I have said, the novels of Lawrence's last phase differ generically from those preceding it. In speaking of imagery, we customarily break it down into image (the thing itself, nothing more), metaphor, and symbol. Most discussions of Lawrence's imagery concentrate upon the first and third categories. Thus Harry T. Moore celebrates the beauty of Lawrence's descriptions, in and for themselves, in such works as *St. Mawr*, *The Plumed Serpent*, and *The Escaped Cock*. Eliseo Vivas, Mark Spilka, and Dorothy Van Ghent, among others, admire the symbolic dimensions of Lawrence's imagery. Spilka analyzes the symbolic ramifications of flower-picking in *Sons and Lovers*, arches in *The Rainbow*, and star-equilibrium in *Women in Love*. Dorothy Van Ghent, in her brilliant analysis of *Sons and Lovers*, writes of Lawrence's method of seeking "the objective equivalent of feeling in the image" and goes on to describe his "great gift for the *symbolic image*" (my italics).[3] In the scenes that Van Ghent focuses upon, the great scenes that all readers remember, there are in fact tremendous symbolic implications in the imagery, but unlike the later fictions, very few metaphors. The following passage, which Van Ghent cites in its entirety, is an example:

> She hurried out of the side garden to the front, where she could stand as if in an immense gulf of white light, the moon streaming high in face of her, the moonlight standing up from the hills in front, and filling the valley where the Bottoms crouched, almost blindingly. There, panting and half weeping in reaction from the stress, she murmured to herself over and over again: "The nuisance! the nuisance!"
>
> She became aware of something about her. With an effort she roused herself to see what it was that penetrated her consciousness. The tall white lilies were reeling in the moonlight, and the air was charged with their perfume, as with a presence. Mrs. Morel gasped slightly in fear. She touched the big, pallid flowers on their petals, then shivered. They seemed to be stretching in the moonlight. She put her hand into one white bin: the gold scarcely showed on her fingers by moonlight. She bent down to look at the binful of yellow pollen; but it only appeared dusky. Then she drank a deep draught of the scent. It almost made her dizzy.
>
> Mrs. Morel leaned on the garden gate, looking out, and she lost herself awhile. She did not know what she thought. Except for a slight

---

2. According to Vivas, the "constitutive symbol" is "considerably more than a matter of intended meaning" (*D. H. Lawrence: The Failure and the Triumph of Art*, 274). He defines it further as "a creative synthesis of empirical matter which manifests itself in dramatic and moral terms and which functions categorically" (275). He cites the "Rabbit" chapter of *Women in Love* as an example.

3. Van Ghent, *The English Novel: Form and Function*, 248.

feeling of sickness, and her consciousness in the child, herself melted out like scent into the shiny, pale air. After a time the child, too, melted with her in the mixing-pot of moonlight, and she rested with the hills and lilies and houses, all swum together in a kind of swoon. (*Sons and Lovers*, 23–24)

The few metaphors are local, not expansive or connective: "the child, too, melted with her"; "the moonlight standing up from the hills"; the "lilies were reeling in the moonlight." These do not play out from the symbols themselves, as the metaphors will in the later fiction, where they will exfoliate into other metaphors, interpenetrate in such a way that they become inseparable from the action.

The same is basically true of *The Rainbow* and *Women in Love*, as I will later have occasion to show. What makes these novels great, among other things, is the way the symbols—or more precisely the symbolic scenes—anticipate and incorporate others. They do so, I believe, primarily through the connective agency of language. Curiously, in the later fiction, it is the longer works, the novels and novellas, in which Lawrence employs this sort of imagery that enables meaning. The stories lack the linguistic density of the novels. They are to the novels as *The Captain's Doll*, written only months before, is to *The Ladybird*: metaphorically spare. It may be that *The Captain's Doll* is the better story. I am not arguing that this narrative strategy is necessarily preferable to another. But although Lawrence did not write another novel achieving the greatness of *Women in Love*, he did achieve a fineness in some of the later works that I think *is* directly attributable to their metaphorical richness, to the organization and depth that the metaphors give them.

Chapter 2

Beginning the Last Phase
Aaron's Rod

Aaron's Rod, in its transitional status, reveals much about Lawrence's narrative methods, as they involve imagery, both before and after that novel. Unfortunately, Lawrence's holograph manuscripts do not exist, though I am not certain we would learn much from them if they did. What is clear is that Lawrence did not revise much, if any, of the first half of *Aaron's Rod* in light of the course taken by the second half, written three or so years later. It is this fact, no doubt, that explains why this novel, in the eyes of most critics, is one of Lawrence's two or three really ugly ducklings. Though *Aaron's Rod* has its defenders, among them John Middleton Murry, F. R. Leavis, and more recently Paul G. Baker, it is those critics like Keith Sagar, who finds it "hollow at its centre," or like Eliseo Vivas, who refers to its "radical incoherence," that form the majority view.[1] Vivas laments the book's structure, which he calls the "formlessness of picaresque," and blames this formlessness on the lack of any organizing symbolic principle:

> The book contains one pseudo-symbol or quasi-symbol, the flute, through which Aaron expresses his spiritual needs, through which he earns his living after leaving his wife, and through which, as might be expected, the obvious Freudian meaning is conveyed. But the symbol is concocted and fails to organize the story. . . . As the golden bowl is central to James's novel, so are water and the moon central to *Women in Love*, bringing together into a concentrated focus the substance of Lawrence's great novel. The flute merely baffles.[2]

That is to say, it baffles Vivas. The reason it baffles, though, is the interesting and essential thing. Vivas is reading the novel and the symbol as he has read novels and symbols in the past. His failure to understand is symptomatic of many readers' failure to understand and properly appreciate the achievement of the later work. Now he must read the confluence of metaphors or systems of imagery that attend the symbol. To be sure, he is partly right. The book does not hang together as it should. Richard Aldington is

---

1. Murry, *D. H. Lawrence: Son of Woman*; Leavis, *D. H. Lawrence: Novelist*; Baker, *A Reassessment of D. H. Lawrence's Aaron's Rod*; Sagar, *The Art of D. H. Lawrence*; Vivas, *D. H. Lawrence: The Failure and the Triumph of Art*.
2. *Failure and Triumph*, 23.

also right when he says the book consists of two essentially unrelated parts.[3] If we look at the first half to see how Lawrence uses the image as symbol and at the second to see how he uses the image primarily as metaphor, we will begin to understand the difference in the two methods and the direction in which Lawrence has begun to move.

Vivas speaks of the novel's one symbol. There are actually two symbols in the first part—neither a flute (the flute does not enter as a symbol until the second half of the novel). These two symbols bring some coherence to the whole, but because they operate essentially in the old way of symbol and do not employ a linking system of metaphor to penetrate very much further into the novel, they are largely unsuccessful.

The first of these, the breaking of the blue Christmas ball by Millicent, Aaron's child, symbolizes the disintegration that is one of the novel's two poles. The ball afterward lies in "fragments, bits." Aaron associates its breaking with the war, which changes "nothing" and yet changes "everything" (12). The process the novel will go on to dramatize is the fragmentation of both the individual and society, as reflected in Rawden Lilly's comment, several chapters later, of the "World coming to pieces bit by bit" (58). Late in the novel, in the passage celebrating the Tuscan cypresses, Aaron reflects that "our [present] life is only a fragment of the shell of life. . . . Much that is life has passed away from men, leaving us all mere bits" (265). Beyond this larger, social meaning, the disintegration of the blue ball images the disintegration of Aaron's marriage and his new life. He must start, that is, from a condition of fragmentation, and work toward integration. Lawrence does not, however, expand this symbol through metaphor to help break down our sense of the discontinuity between the earlier and later parts of the novel, as he will expand the symbol of the flute. When Lawrence toward the end has Aaron reflect on men's fragmentariness, he neglects (perhaps *he* has forgotten, as the reader probably has) to make the organizing connection with the ball. The symbol, then, fails to constitute or organize.

The same may be said of the second symbol, the Christmas tree, whose cleverness is almost totally wasted. It figures in a scene that slyly epitomizes the opposition of polarities and anticipates Aaron's symbolic dimensions as a disoriented modern Pan. We remember that Jim Bricknell, his fiancée Josephine Ford, his sister Julia, her husband Robert Cunningham, and a young man named Cyril Scott, out of boredom on Christmas eve, leave the ugly Bricknell house (built through the profits of industrialism) and begin to affix candles to a fir tree on the lawn. It is merely an amusement for them. But Lawrence's description of the scene has a deliberate

3. Introduction to the Penguin edition of *Aaron's Rod*, 8–9.

mythic dimension to it. Julia says, "We ought to do a ritual dance! We ought to worship the tree" (32). We tend not to pay much attention to her gushings, but we should. Indeed, as a group they are patently representative of the "dead, mechanical ideal" gripping English life. They embody the process by which England and the "north" in general have gone wrong by falling away from the "spontaneous life-dynamic." They number, these individuals, among that large host of Lawrencian characters who have lost "connection." Lawrence describes the scene in this way:

> The beam of the bicycle lamp moved and fell upon the hands and faces of the young people, and penetrated the recesses of the secret trees. Several little tongues of flame clipped sensitive and ruddy on the naked air, sending a faint glow over the needle foliage. They gave a strange, perpendicular aspiration in the night. Julia waved slowly in her tree dance. Jim stood apart, with his legs straddled, a motionless figure.
>
> The party round the tree became absorbed and excited as more ruddy tongues of flame pricked upward from the dark tree. Pale candles became evident, the air was luminous. The illumination was becoming complete, harmonious.
>
> Josephine suddenly looked round.
>
> "Why-y-y!" came her long note of alarm.
>
> A man in a bowler hat and a black overcoat stood on the edge of the twilight.
>
> "What is it?" cried Julia.
>
> "*Homo sapiens*!" said Robert, the lieutenant. "Hand the light, Cyril."
>
> He played the beam of light full on the intruder: a man in a bowler hat, with a black overcoat buttoned to his throat, a pale, dazed, blinking face. The hat was tilted at a slightly jaunty angle over the left eye, the man was well-featured. He did not speak.
>
> "Did you want anything?" asked Robert, from behind the light.
>
> Aaron Sisson blinked, trying to see who addressed him. To him they were all illusory. He did not answer.
>
> "Anything you wanted?" repeated Robert, military, rather peremptory.
>
> Jim suddenly doubled himself up and burst into a loud harsh cackle of laughter. (33)

It is a masterly scene. Julia's dance is an unconscious parody, and Robert's "*Homo sapiens*" is true in a way neither he nor the others can begin to perceive. Though his knowledge may be inarticulate, undeveloped, Aaron is the one who truly knows. That the figures are "illusory" to him is symbolically appropriate: they are not real; they do not exist. They have managed, by tricking up the fir with lights and through Julia's little travesty of a ritual dance, to conjure the god of the woods. And he does not see them! The irony goes deeper. Not only are they illusory, they also get the Pan that they deserve—a comical-looking, bewildered fellow in a dark suit and rakishly tilted bowler hat. No wonder Jim begins laughing and the rest follow. This laughter, like the other details, is symbolic; their attitude toward the values the book endorses is merely one of facetious amusement. Lawrence is near the top of his form—at least his satiric form—in his management of this episode. But because Lawrence does not make connections, the effect quickly dissipates. The mythic dimension, which comes through so successfully in later works like *St. Mawr*, *Lady Chatterley's Lover*, and *The Escaped Cock*, is simply allowed to peter out after its brief evocation here. Had Lawrence written these two scenes in 1921 and not in 1917, I do not think that he would have been content to let them be. He would have found metaphors to amplify them. As they are, they fail to resonate, and the reader has trouble hearing them.

One does hear the flute, however—provided one listens carefully. If its sound fails to carry, it is because the story's talkiness or apparently picaresque development distracts, or it is because previous novels have not prepared one to hear it. The imagery attendant on the flute is significant in the development of the action, as it will be in the longer fiction after *Aaron's Rod*.

However, as I have mentioned, Vivas contends that, for all its presence, the flute still "fails to organize the story." It baffles him because he fails to understand its connection with the book's other images. Like many others who dislike the novel, he seems unaware that there is any other imagery or that this imagery *does* anything. Moreover, if we see only the Freudian aspects of the rod as Vivas does, we miss its primary meaning and function. Primarily it is a symbol of organic life, and as such its several exfoliations bring the imagery as a whole into organic relation. How diverse, how expansive, this imagery is and how it synthesizes the action of the novel, at least its second half, are the concerns of the remainder of this chapter.

Aaron's rod figures twice in the Old Testament: in Exodus 7:10 Aaron casts the rod before Pharaoh and it turns into a serpent; later, in Numbers 17:8, it blossoms. "Aaron's rod" is also a plant that flowers upon a long stem. Lawrence here is chiefly interested in its flowering aspect (though in his fiction after *Aaron's Rod* the snake becomes a central metaphor). But what does the flowering aspect have to do with Aaron's quest? Or with a thematic statement like the following obviously central one?

> His [Aaron's] intrinsic and central aloneness was the very centre of his being. Break it, and he broke his being. Break this central aloneness, and he broke everything. It was the great temptation, to yield himself: and it was the final sacrilege. Anyhow, it was something which, from his profoundest soul, he did not intend to do. By the innermost isolation and singleness of his own soul he would abide though the skies fell on top of one another, and seven heavens collapsed. (162)

We begin to see the relationship if we reexamine a conversation that takes place about thirty pages earlier. Dining in Novara with the Franks, Aaron has asserted his preference for pure melody. But Lady Franks responds, "But you can't mean that you would like all music to go back to melody pure and simple! Just a flute—just a pipe! Oh, Mr. Sisson, you are bigoted for your instrument. I just *live* in harmony—chords, chords!" (136).

Throughout the latter half of the novel, music serves as a metaphor for the Lawrencian ethic of singleness. The Marchesa shares Aaron's detestation of chords, of "musical notes . . . come together, harmonies or discords" (225). When she begins at last to sing again after her long silence, she sings to the accompaniment of the single instrument of Aaron's flute. It is like a bird's singing, but unlike "in that the notes followed clear and single." It is a "wild" sound, like a nightingale's: "To read all the human pathos into nightingales' singing is nonsense. A wild, savage, non-human lurch and squander of sound . . . . " (227). It is too bad for Aaron, of course, that the Marchesa does not work out very much better for him than Lottie, who also does not want to leave him free and single in his male power, but wishes to domineer over it. Nonetheless, Aaron has already begun to find what will partially suffice for him: Italy, in particular Florence—and Lilly.

Vivas charges specifically that Aaron's desertion of his wife lacks credibility because Aaron's frustrations are not dramatized and more generally that there is "no organic relation between characters and ideas."[4] The first criticism can be answered easily enough by showing how Aaron's later behavior and thoughts account for his earlier actions. The second charge is potentially the more damaging one. But it will not hold: an organic relation does obtain between characters and ideas. And it does so as these characters and ideas are constituted in and developed through the imagery.

Let us consider, for instance, Aaron's flute in more detail. Lawrence calls it Aaron's "black rod of power." But he does not stop at this. When Aaron leaves the Marchesa's following her revelation that she can sing again, Aaron returns home "newly flushed with his own male super-power, he was going to have his reward" (257):

> And now came his desire back. But strong, fierce as iron. Like the strength of an eagle with the lightning in its talons. Something to glory in, something overweening, the powerful male passion, arrogant, royal, Jove's thunderbolt. Aaron's black rod of power, blossoming again with red Florentine lilies and fierce thorns. He moved about in the splendour of his own male lightning, invested in the thunder of the male passion-power. He had got it back, the male godliness, the male godhead. (258)

4. *Failure and Triumph*, 35.

The images that stand out here are the fierce eagle and the red Florentine lily. Each is connected with Aaron's "rod of power" and thereby with each other. But neither is a new image. They are components in a complex of separate images that resonate one with the other, again and again. For example, the eagle first appears in the passage describing Lawrence's love ideal: "Two eagles in mid-air, maybe, like Whitman's 'Dalliance of Eagles.' Two eagles in mid-air, grappling, whirling, coming to their intensification of love-oneness there in mid-air" (166–67). In the first part of the paragraph, we find nothing less than an extended metaphor involving a lily:

> The long fight with Lottie had driven him at last to himself, so that he was quiet as a thing which has its root deep in life, and has lost its anxiety. As for considering the lily, it is not a matter of consideration. The lily toils and spins hard enough, in her own way. But without that strain and that anxiety with which we try to weave ourselves a life. The lily is life-rooted, life-central. She *cannot* worry. She is life itself, a little, delicate fountain playing creatively, for as long or as short a time as may be, and unable to be anxious. She may be sad or sorry, if the north wind blows. But even then, anxious she cannot be. Whether her fountain play or cease to play, from out the cold, damp earth, she cannot be anxious. She may only be glad or sorry, and continue her way. She is perfectly herself, whatever befall! even if frosts cut her off. Happy lily, never to be saddled with an *idée fixe*, never to be in the grip of a monomania for happiness or love or fulfillment. It is not *laisser aller*. It is life-rootedness. It is being by oneself, life-living, like the much-mooted lily. One toils, one spins, one strives: just as the lily does. But like her, taking one's own life-way amidst everything, and taking one's own life-way alone. Love too. (166)

Leading into the eagle trope, this quotation begins with a reference to Lottie. The eagle-lily-flute-male power quotation was inspired in the first place by Aaron's thoughts about the Marchesa. We progress from character to character, idea to further development of idea, through the linkage of metaphors which, we begin to realize, must be more than coincidental. The lily image, moreover, means that Lilly, whose name is hardly accidental and toward whose ethic Aaron more nearly navigates than gravitates during the course of the action, is implicitly present throughout the novel. In this passage Lawrence also connects the lily with a fountain ("whether her fountain play, or cease to play"), providing another "life" image and anticipating, perhaps, Aaron's final action in throwing the flute into the river, where it will resurrect.

As becomes increasingly apparent, Lawrence's method is to use not one but a combination of images. We make associations with previous combinations so as to form a network that draws within the sphere of its influence characters, scenes, and ideas otherwise existing in a picaresque limbo. But the imagery catches them up and puts them within a frame. The scene in which Aaron and Lilly are sitting on Argyle's loggia in Florence also demonstrates how this is done:

> Sunlight, lovely full sunlight, lingered warm and still on the balcony. It caught the façade of the cathedral sideways, like the tips of a flower, and sideways lit up the stem of Giotto's tower, like a lily stem, or a long, lovely pale pink and white and green pistil of the lily of the cathedral. Florence, the flowery town. Firenze—Fiorenze—the flowery town: the red lilies. The Fiorentini, the flower-souled. Flowers with good roots in the mud and muck, as should be: and fearless blossoms in air, like the cathedral and the tower and the David. (232)

The last is a reference to the statues in the Piazza della Signoria, where Aaron felt a new life starting in him. In this passage the tower, through its phallic suggestiveness, provokes natural associations with Aaron's rod—with Florence, too, through its name and through its identification with the lilies, since the flute is said in that earlier passage to blossom with red lilies. Lilly establishes the identifications further when he speaks of his love for the tower with its "dark stripes . . . like the tiger marks on a pink lily." He calls it "a lily, not a rose: a pinky white lily with dark tigery marks." He concludes that "here men for a moment were themselves, as a plant in flower is for the moment completely itself" (232)—as Lilly is and Aaron is striving to be. The images direct our attention to previous passages, leading us to make the proper connections, such as those between Giotto's tower and Aaron's rod. When Aaron first arrived in Florence, his flute would not "blossom" (210). When he throws the broken flute into the Arno near the end, in the chapter that artistically should be the last, Lilly soothes him, telling him that it will "grow again. It's a reed, a water-plant—you can't kill it" (285).

The flute, then, is organic, like the metaphors that work within the novel by flowering one from another. The new image in the description of the tower is the tiger-marks. But again, is it new really? In point of fact, Lawrence described the mountains about Novara, the previous city, as tigers. Aaron felt awe before the "white-fanged mountains" (151) in the distance, "the tiger-like Alps. Tigers prowling between the north and south" (150). The metaphor connects the episodes, but more importantly, it advances the ideas of the "spontaneous life-dynamic," which in Lawrence's symbolism is the "south" pole of our being, to be approached if not fulfilled later through Aaron's black rod of power, whose red lily blossoms are streaked with "tigery" marks. Image sprouts image, sometimes literally; the result is a satisfying internal coherence.

In a broken world, one seeks both what has not yet been broken and what will restore. After sleeping with the Marchesa and finding her to be, like Lottie, willfully resistant to the male authority in him, Aaron finds escape the next day in the Tuscan woods among the cypresses. Here he has his realization that "our life is only a fragment of the shell of life. That there has been and will be life, human life such as we do not begin to conceive. Much that is life has passed away from men, leaving us all mere bits" (265). But the cypresses, in the "mindful silence," contain "lost human ways of feeling and of knowing." They hold "great life realities gone into the darkness." Aaron feels that "the cypresses commemorate." He is aware of them "rising dark about him, like so many high visitants from an old, lost, lost subtle world, where men had the wonder of demons about them" (265). Here, though none of the earlier imagery is present, the erect demonic trees are another manifestation of Aaron's flute, his rod of male authority with its regenerative, organic properties. The description also suggests Blake's "forests of the night," thick with the "tigers of wrath." Moreover, the tree image importantly links the episode with the later scene in which Lilly tells Aaron how to be: "You thought there was something outside, to justify you: God, or a creed, or a prescription. But remember, your soul inside you is your only Godhead. It develops your actions within you as a tree develops its own new cells." The mode for living, of course, is organic, as the imagery has prepared us to expect it would be. Lilly then tells Aaron, in a figure which embraces by association the previous flute and lily tropes, that these "cells push on into buds and boughs and flowers" (296). For finally, "you are your own Tree of Life, roots and limbs and trunk." This tree contains the "Holy Ghost," which "puts forth new buds, and pushes past old limits, and shakes off a whole body of dying leaves. And the old limits hate being empassed, and the old leaves hate to fall. But they must, if the tree-soul says so" (296). Thus, it is not so bad a thing, as Lilly has earlier told Aaron, for the flute to be smashed. We can see that it has to be if the Holy Ghost in Aaron, paralleling the exfoliating actions of the flute, is to sprout new leaves and flowers. Lawrence has so managed the imagery to this point that this conversation, through the metaphors, now picks up and advances previous conversations and ideas. Talky though this novel is, its ideas achieve a dramatic force by virtue of the imagery. Giotto's tower, the commemorative cypresses, the blossoming, and later the broken flute—these do more than reinforce. They create, in good measure, the meaning.

The action in the novel's second part, it seems, has been embedded all along in the imagery. Significantly too, as we have observed, the imagery has been embedded *in the imagery*. But to make all the connections requires an imaginative leap that it is unfair to ask of the reader. Moreover, Lawrence has not earned all of them. However inchoate, they are there nonetheless. The broken blue Christmas ball becomes the broken ebony flute. These are each religious symbols. The breaking of the blue ball signifies in part the disintegration or perversion of time-honored traditional values, especially when we think of this scene in relation to the Christmas-tree scene at the Bricknell's. The broken rod, the shattered panpipe, signifies the triumph of mechanistic functionalism over the "spontaneous life-ideal." That is, the modern tendency to disintegration or fragmentation sweeps before it the ancient (including medieval: hence Giotto's tower) ideal of organic integration. But this is yet not the whole story. The symbols have more than one facet. The shattering of first the Christmas ball and then the flute marks stages in Aaron's self-overcoming, or rebirth. As Lilly tells him, the tree-soul has to shake off a "whole body of dying leaves" in order to renew itself—much as Aaron's rod must be broken in order to blossom again. The rod is an extraordinarily embracing or "enabling" image, as I will use that term in the next chapter. It fuses the two polar forces of the novel, disintegration and integration. In doing so it connects the major and most of the minor developments of the novel. For Tommy Dukes in *Lady Chatterley's Lover*, the phallus was civilization's saving "bridge"; for this novel, Aaron's rod achieves a similar organic result. Its associations—and in several instances identifications—with just about every other important image bring the several actions of the novel within a coherent frame, as the interpenetrating metaphors of *Lady Chatterley's Lover* authenticate, organize meaningfully, Tommy Dukes's statement within a dramatic context.

Aaron's Rod does not achieve the same measure of success managed by *Lady Chatterley's Lover* through its first three-quarters. In Lawrence's best fiction of this last period, myth and metaphor nourish and signify one another from almost the opening pages. If *Aaron's Rod* is only partially successful (though considerably more successful than many would allow), it is still among Lawrence's most interesting works since it originates the method that makes the novels of this last phase distinctively rewarding.

Chapter 3

The Ladybird and the Enabling Image

"In our own wild nature we find the best recreation from our
un-nature, from our spirituality."

Nietzsche, *Twilight of the Idols*

To appreciate fully the rewards that *The Ladybird* has to offer, one
must approach it through the dimension of its imagery; there, as with
Aaron's Rod, the reader finds its distinctiveness. Lawrence, writing to Middleton Murry, said that he thought *The Ladybird* had "more the quick of a
new thing" (*Letters*, 4:447) than either *The Fox* or *The Captain's Doll*.[1]
Interestingly, at the time that Lawrence completed the other two stories, he
wrote to Seltzer that " 'The Fox' and 'The Captain's Doll' are so modern, so
new: a new manner" (*Letters*, 4:132). It was only later, when he was well
into his new method, that he fully recognized its originality. Since a majority of those Lawrence critics who have written about the novella do not
much like it, Lawrence's statement must bemuse them.[2] Graham Hough,
for instance, calls the work a "failure," full of the kind of "pseudomystical
vapouring" present in *The Plumed Serpent*. Julian Moynahan thinks it
Lawrence's "ugliest story," issuing from "the same unwholesome region of
Lawrence's imagination in which the leadership novels have developed."
Count Dionys, Moynahan cannot resist saying, is a "lineal descendent of
Dracula except that, like Bela Lugosi, he stultifies when he intends to
thrill." So much, seemingly, for "quickness." F. R. Leavis, though he believes the opening and middle portions to be "remarkable achievements,"
also considers the ending a failure, an "evasion that conjures away the
actual world and its difficulties." Not all critics, to be sure, agree that the
story fails. Monroe Engle and James C. Cowan give the story sympathetic
and neutral readings respectively, though neither discussion centers in the
"art" of the story.[3] My own view is that *The Ladybird*, whatever its merits

1. All three stories were brought together in the collection entitled *The Ladybird*, published in 1923.
2. Indeed, *The Ladybird* has been neglected in Lawrence criticism. In book-length
studies of Lawrence's fiction, the story is fortunate when it gets more than a page or two of
treatment, and this treatment usually dismissive. Of articles, there are but a handful. No one
attempts a serious consideration of the story's "art."
3. Hough, *The Dark Sun: A Study of D. H. Lawrence*, 176; Moynahan, *The Deed of Life:*

in relation to, say, *The Captain's Doll*, is nonetheless successful on its own terms and is at least as interesting in its artistic dimensions (*more* interesting in this regard than either of the other stories) as in its ideas, which are the focus of most of the criticism.

To understand why Lawrence believed the story to contain this "quick of a new thing,"[4] we only have to recall the longer fiction Lawrence had written since *Women in Love*. He had published two novels, *The Lost Girl* (1920) and *Aaron's Rod*, and he had just completed the second version of *The Fox* and *The Captain's Doll* when he began *The Ladybird* in December, 1921. Of these several works, as we have seen, *Aaron's Rod* is the only one that attempts anything approaching a texture of imagery and symbol. *The Lost Girl* is almost entirely straightforward, naturalistic narrative, effectively devoid of metaphor or symbol other than the purely local variety. Though both contain important symbols, *The Fox* and *The Captain's Doll*, similarly, work almost entirely on the surface of language. Not so *The Ladybird*: Lawrence's language here is densely metaphorical. So different is it in this respect that Lawrence must have thought indeed that here was "the quick of a new thing." *The Ladybird* is a novella about surfaces and subsurfaces, and to appreciate what Lawrence meant in his statement to Murry, the reader has to be alert to the subsurfaces of the narrative, which one enters through the imagery. This is the work whose strategy of language, involving as it does an extensive organization of metaphorical under-meanings, anticipates the central narrative strategies of Lawrence's three final full-length novels and the two outstanding novellas.

This strategy informs *The Ladybird*, unlike *Aaron's Rod*, for the reasons we have seen, almost from the beginning. Lawrence describes Daphne as having "a wild energy dammed up inside her" (*Lady Bird*, 47) that belies her blond, pale, even phthisic beauty. Though she is a "daredevil," like her Scottish father, Lord Beveridge, her mind, adopting her mother's "spiritual" creed, hates daredevils: "So, her reckless, anti-philanthropic passion could find no outlet—and *should* find no outlet, she thought. So her own blood turned against her, beat on her own nerves, and destroyed her." Though her will is set in its belief "that life should be gentle and good and benevolent," her blood, on the other hand, "had its revenge on her. So it is with strong natures today: shattered from the

***

The Novels and Tales of D. H. Lawrence, 178; Leavis, *D. H. Lawrence: Novelist*, 66; Engle, "The Continuity of D. H. Lawrence's Short Novels"; Cowan, *D. H. Lawrence's American Journey: A Study in Literature and Myth*.

4. When Lawrence makes this statement in the Murry letter, he goes on to say that *The Fox* belongs "more to the old world." Since he is writing from Mexico, we can hardly doubt that the "new thing" refers at least in part to the "New World" experience that in his fiction culminates in the failure of *The Plumed Serpent*. But "the quick" implies something more nearly relating to the way the story is *rendered*.

inside" (47). What the reader notices first, correctly of course, is the antagonism between the mind and the blood. This is the ever-present conflict in Lawrence. Less apparent, working from underneath, is the dualistic pattern of inside-outside that leaves its impressions just below the surface, or external, level of the action. Thus, the wild energy is dammed up *inside* her; it can find no *outlet*, should find no *outlet*, so it is destroyed from the *inside*. Cowan, largely working from Nietzsche's *The Birth of Tragedy*, gives the best discussion of the story's most obvious external dimension (and its most immediately illuminating one), the Dionysian-Apollonian duality:

> The Apollonian tradition, concerned with exterior objects that occupy linear space or with externalized mental conceptions, elevates as 'real' that mode of perception characterized by the objectifying intellect. The ideal of intellectual beauty becomes, then, the rational faculty, making analytical discriminations in the conscious mind. In this mode, the intellectual seeker detaches himself from the subjective to project himself in quest of the light of truth in the outer world. . . . The Dionysian tradition, on the contrary, concerned with interior perceptions, elevates as 'real' that mode of perception characterized by the creative imagination. . . . In this mode, the intellectual seeker incorporates elements of the outer world into the inner world, to seek the truth darkly by plunging into the cyclic night within the self.[5]

Lawrence obviously has this Apollonian-Dionysian opposition in mind in this opposing of the blond Basil and the dark, little Dionys. I do not want to go into all the details of this opposition and the way in which Lawrence develops them (Cowan explicates this quite nicely), but rather wish to consider how Lawrence builds *under* his external structures. In the above quotations from the story, we see the way that the language grows naturally out of the meanings ("inner," "outlet," "inside") appropriate to the external and internal aspects of the Apollonian and the Dionysian modes. I wish to show that Lawrence *artistically* exploits these outward and inward dimensions of the two modes through a language whose symbolic details and metaphors reinforce, subterraneously as it were, the surface meanings. Lawrence's motive for metaphor here is to provide, as Emily Dickinson put it, "internal difference, where the meanings are"—that is, the real ones. So Lawrence, highly aware, as any good artist is, of the

---

5. Cowan, *American Journey*, 77–78. For the explanation of Apollonian-Dionysian polarity, I have quoted Cowan at length here, rather than Nietzsche, to indicate how a Lawrence scholar, though himself not concerned with imagery, nonetheless uses the terms ("exterior objects," "externalized mental conceptions," "outer world," "interior perceptions," "inner world") that embrace it.

organic relation between form and content, would have it in *The Ladybird*.

The main outside-inside opposition works off several others that are for the most part synecdoches of one another and for the main pair. These include over-under (height-depth), light-dark, and exposed-hidden tropes. These polarities involve imagery of flowers, animals, water, earth, names, bodily organs, class, time, sun, moon, heaven, and hell. For the most part, Lawrence orchestrates these unobtrusively, bringing them into contexts where they resonate. And resonance is a good deal of the meaning as well as a way of explaining how the metaphors operate.

Lawrence's strategy with the names of his characters indicates quite early the difference between this novella and the other two. A more "clever" Lawrence is at work in *The Ladybird*. Daphne is not what her name implies: "But Daphne was not born for grief and philanthropy. With her splendid frame, and her lovely, long, strong legs, she was Artemis or Atalanta rather than Daphne" (47). To be sure, as Basil's (Apollo's) wife, she is Daphne. And in the day, even after Dionys ("I have no power in the day," he tells her [104]), she will be Daphne. But with her interior "wild energy" she is Artemis, or Atalanta, not the shrinking virgin Daphne in flight from phallic love.[6] As we shall see, however, in becoming Count Psanek's lover, Daphne becomes not an Artemis or an Atalanta, but another mythic personage. But at this moment in the story, this Daphne, *inside*, is far from being that someone else. The Daphne aspect of this inner being (call it for now Atalanta) is superficial merely, unreal; or if we read the story purely in terms of the Nietzschean synthesis of the Apollonian and the Dionysian, the exterior Daphne self has little meaning or force until it comes into relation with its interior counterpart, the "dark" Dionysian sister within.

The case of the Count is somewhat different. His full name is Johann Dionys Psanek. Early in the story, still near death from his wounds, he tells Daphne that he wishes to be Johann Dionys no longer, but Karl or Wilhelm or Ernst or George. The Johann Dionys is "shot away" (53), another way of saying that the war has nearly destroyed him internally, as it also nearly destroys the inner being of Richard Lovat Somers in *Kangaroo*. Possibly significant is the burying of "Dionys" between "Johann" and "Psanek," the Dionysian being the hidden, instinctual self. Along the same lines of strategy are the anagrams and buried words in Psanek. As Cowan has observed, Psanek contains the anagrams of both snake and asp (82). We are seeing in *The Ladybird* the first phase of Lawrence's interest for fictional

---

6. Actually, as we can see, the names do not quite work for Lawrence. The urgent Apollo from whom the mythic Daphne flees is not the same "light" Apollo who figures in Nietzsche's Apollonian-Dionysian polarity. Moreover, it is Dionys, in the story, whom she initially fears and is in flight from, though finally he is less the chaser than the chased.

purposes in the snake as a symbolic image in his ethos.[7] At the winter solstice, Dionysus assumed the form of a snake; appropriately, therefore, on the thimble the Count had given Daphne years before, a snake encircles the base. Like the ladybird also represented on the thimble, the snake lives underground, in the *underworld*. *Psanek*, however contains not only *snake* and *asp*, but also (Cowan fails to mention) *Pan* and *sane*. Certainly it is the Pan aspect of Dionysus that attracts Lawrence, not the bibulous aspect more usually suggested by his Roman name. As for *sane*, we have only to recall the poet's observation that "Much madness is divinest sense"; Dickinson's meaning is almost precisely Lawrence's as well. In the external world the Count is insane. But for Lawrence, as his fiction of the period increasingly predicates, the external world itself is mad and therefore requires destruction. True sanity is to be located only within the inner self, as the word *sane* is located within *Psanek*. It is a divine sanity, too—hence *Dionys*, the god. But such sanity is always outside the law of the external world; consequently, the Bohemian meaning of Psanek, "outlaw." Outside the law is *inside* the individual. The number of *in* words seems to multiply as we watch Lawrence's technique in the story taking shape. The point that these words make, again and again, is the internalness of sanity. Thus, after Daphne has been with Dionys in his room, we are told, "She was so still inside her" (107). Dionys tells Basil, "A man can only be happy following his inmost need" (109). Though probably not deliberate, the accumulation of *in* words reinforces the meaning; sanity derives not from without as Lady Beveridge seeks it, but from within, as Lady Daphne at last comes to discover it. Surely deliberate, though, is the story's texture of metaphor, of synecdoche, as in the instance of the Count's name. Just as certain tones bring out other tones, Lawrence orchestrates the details in the story so that they build upon and advance, or *enable*, one another. Certainly it is this quality that marks *The Ladybird* as different from *The Fox* and *The Captain's Doll*, whose few metaphors are chiefly local. *The Ladybird* at last is an elaborate and consistently orchestrated conceit.

Throughout the story, it is what is under, or in, or behind, that signifies—whatever is concealed from public view. At the beginning, Dionys lies in his hospital bed, almost dead: "His face seemed to Daphne curiously hidden behind the black beard" (51). On a later visit, Daphne looks at "the flesh through his beard, as water through reeds" (58). He tells her that there is "a devil in my body that will not die." This devil keeps him alive. The detail resonates with that of the snake in "Psanek." (Of course,

---

7. See Sagar, *D. H. Lawrence: Life into Art*, 201, 234–36, for the development of Lawrence's interest in the snake as a symbol.

Daphne has also repressed a "daredevil" within her.) When he is able to get up and they go out, he "seemed to keep inside his own reserves," to put "a shadow between himself and [the other prisoners], and from across this shadow he looked with his dark, beautifully-fringed eyes, as a proud little beast from the shadow of its lair" (59). Within, then, are devil and beast, which are perhaps the same, together with a third presence that I shall come to.

Daphne, on her side, is "like a flower behind a rock, near an icy water" (55), as Dionys puts it at the beginning. This is a criticism: "You do not live too much." But as the story goes on to argue, some degree of concealment is a necessary condition of living, of survival. Later, of course, in *The Plumed Serpent*, toward which the ideas and method of *The Ladybird* are moving, the serpent comes out of its hiding—but not convincingly. By definition the "descendental" must remain below, the *in*stinctual with*in*. The flower image here is instructive of the story's manner with imagery: just as the flower opens to something deeper inside, so the image itself opens more deeply into further images, leading the reader like an initiate (Dionys tells Daphne that he is an "initiate . . . to secret knowledge" [66]) from the surface region of the story to its internal and, in another sense, infernal region. Thus, from the preceding image Lawrence moves us to this one: "Her wide, green-blue eyes seemed like the heart of some curious, full-open flower" (58). Now with flower we have eyes and heart. A scene or two later (Basil still has not returned from the war), Daphne is sitting alone before a mirror: "And she looked at her blue-green eyes—the eyes of the wildcat on a bough. Yes, the lovely bluegreen iris drawn tight like a screen. Supposing it should relax. Supposing it should *unfold*, and *open out* the dark depths, the dark, dilated pupil! Supposing it should?" (69; my italics). In the previous scene, she had looked into Dionys's eyes: "She could see the darkness swaying in the depths. She perceived the invisible, cat-like fire stirring deep inside them, felt it coming towards her" (68). Then she had to turn aside her face. Though she does not at this point "like" Dionys, we see the "dark depths" in her responding to those in him. The point is that, proceeding from isolated images, Lawrence has created a meaning-making constellation of them.

The image and concept of the "dark sun" is implicit in each of the preceding passages. In some writers and perhaps occasionally in Lawrence, the complexity is deceiving: there is finally less than meets the eye. But here, I think, the simplicity of the imagery deceives. So much is contained in these lines and so much has prepared for them. For instance, when Daphne first goes to see Dionys, the following, seemingly insignificant byplay occurs before we get to Dionys's revelation that he is a "fire-worshipper":

> Suddenly his dark eyes opened and caught her looking.
> "The sun makes even anger open like a flower," he said.
> "Whose anger?" she said.
> "I don't know. But I can make flowers, looking through my eye-lashes. Do you know how?"
> "You mean rainbows?"
> "Yes, flowers."
> And she saw him, with a curious smile on his lips, looking through his almost closed eyelids at the sun.
> "The sun is neither English nor German nor Bohemian," he said. "I am a subject of the sun. I belong to the fire-worshippers." (57)

To her puzzled "You mean rainbows?" his "Yes, flowers" must appear as a sort of misunderstanding or confusion consonant with the gravity of his mental and physical state. In reality, it prepares for the description of Daphne's "blue-green iris drawn tight" about, perhaps, to "unfold, and open out the dark depths, the dark, dilated pupil!" The image of the iris embraces three ideas, three previous images: the rainbow, Lawrence's symbol of resurrection; the flower with its unfolding; and as it encircles the dilating pupil, the dark sun that is beginning its growth and fire in Daphne's "dark depths."

At her previous visit to Dionys, prior to the scene in which she looks in the mirror, he tells her of the secret society to which the members of his family have always been initiates:

> "This is what I was taught. The true fire is invisible. Flame, and the red fire we see burning, has its back to us. It is running away from us. Does that mean anything to you?"
> "Yes."
> "Well then, the yellowness of sunshine—light itself—that is only the glancing aside of the real original fire. You know that is true. There would be no light if there was no refraction, no bits of dust and stuff to turn the dark fire into visibility. You know that's a fact. And that being so, even the sun is dark. It is only his jacket of dust that makes him visible. You know that too. And the true sunbeams coming towards us flow darkly, a moving darkness of the genuine fire. The sun is dark, the sunshine flowing to us is dark. And light is only the inside-turning away of the sun's directness that was coming to us. Does that interest you at all?"
> "Yes," she said dubiously.
> "Well, we've got the world inside out. The true living world of fire is dark, throbbing, darker than blood. Our luminous world that we go by is only the reverse of this."
> "Yes, I like that," she said.
> "Well! Now listen. The same with love. This white love that we have is the same. It is only the reverse, the whited sepulchre of the true love. True love is dark, a throbbing together in darkness, like the wild-cat in the night, when the green screen opens and her eyes are on the darkness.
> "No, I don't see that," she said in a slow, clanging voice.
> "You, and your beauty—that is only the inside-out of you. The real

> you is the wild-cat invisible in the night, with red fire perhaps coming out
> of its wide, dark eyes. Your beauty is your whited sepulchre." (67)

The wildcat, which Daphne is to begin to see in her own eyes, is, of course, one of those creatures of hiding. Earlier Dionys had said that even these creatures find their mates. In fact, "Everything finds its mate. . . . One thinks so often that only the dove and the nightingale and the stag with his antlers have gentle mates. And a white she-bear with her cubs under a rock as a snake lies hidden. . . ." (58) The two levels on which these passages work are clear: the external level, that of the plot, forecasting the affair of Dionys and Daphne at her father's estate in Scotland; and the internal level of the real, central action, which resides predominately in the undercurrents of meaning carried by the images. The fire, or sun, becomes the third aspect or dimension that I mentioned earlier, the element joining with devil and beast (snake, wildcat, ladybug) to form a tri-une inner self within Dionys. Each overlays the other. We see the elemental and necessary unity of Lawrence's design especially when we think of the beast part or serpent (though wildcat, similar to Blake's tiger, will do). The demon exists to destroy; the ladybird, the work's main symbol, as the "principle of decomposition," is also the "creative principle" (97). Thus, when Dionys tells Daphne of his desire to pull things down in order to build them again, the "devil" becomes the "god of destruction. The blessed god of destruction. . . . The god of anger, who throws down the steeples and the factory chimneys" (73–74). Earlier, through another connecting image, Dionys had told Daphne to let her anger grow, to "make friends" with it: "That is the way to let your beauty blossom" (65).

It is not her beauty, however, that he cares about. Being external, it is only a "whited sepulchre." In the "world inside-out," the one we must nurture, something other than physical beauty matters since the outside world is to be torn down anyway. In sentences that betray a further debt to Nietzsche, who is constantly present in the story though unacknowledged, Lawrence has Dionys say, "I believe in the power of my red, dark heart. God has put the hammer in my breast—the little eternal hammer," whose business it is "to destroy the world of man" (74).[8] Once again a flower

---

8. The influence of Nietzsche upon *The Ladybird*, as my epigraph would suggest, stretches considerably beyond the story's Apollonian-Dionysian polarity. The idea of Dionys's "hammer," though not attributed, is clearly taken from Nietzsche's *Twilight of the Idols*, whose subtitle is *How One Philosophizes with a Hammer*. The concluding passage of *Twilight*, lifted verbatim from *Thus Spoke Zarathustra* (326), is given the heading "The Hammer Speaks" (563). We can also see why Lawrence gave Dionys his last name of Psanek. Zarathustra asks, " 'Whom do they hate most?' The *creator* they hate most: he breaks tablets and old values. He is a breaker, they call him lawbreaker" (324): an *outlaw*, in short. Earlier in *Zarathustra*: "I teach you the overman. The overman *shall be* the meaning of the earth. I beseech you my

image serves to make the point about the outside-inside difference. Dionys tells Daphne that he "knows" her: "Not the white plucked lily of your body. I have gathered no flower for my ostentatious life. But in the cold dark, your lily root, Lady Daphne. Ah, yes, you will know it all your life, that I know where your root lies buried, with its sad, sad quick of life" (75). Not the flower that blossoms, however beautifully, *outside*, but the buried root *inside* is what matters. "The Crown" posited a balance between lion and unicorn, blood and mind knowledge, and this story in its division of Daphne between Dionys and Apollo-Basil might appear to posit the same. But the imagery says otherwise. The lion, or wildcat as the case may be, has *all* the "quick" about it. In a world that needs tearing down, the red heart, or beast, or hammer within takes precedence over the unicorn's mildness. It is the root that nourishes the flower.

Although the story is not divided into parts, Basil's return, coming about midpoint, marks a natural division in the action—and a new direction in the imagery. Insideness-outsideness remains the unifying concept, but it is translated now, until the last phase of the story, largely in terms of verticality and color. After Basil returns, Daphne becomes ill again. His "adoration-lust" takes its toll upon her nerves. The following passage exhibits her strain in the language of both sorts of imagery: "That fierce power of being alone, even with your lover, the fierce power of the woman *in excelsis*—alas, she could not keep it. She could rise to the height for the time, the incandescent, transcendent, moon-fierce womanhood. But alas, she could not stay intensified and resplendent in her white, womanly powers, her female mystery" (82). In a phrase that captures the absolute oppositions of the story, Basil tells Dionys (Daphne has taken her husband to meet him at the hospital) that Daphne has been "the one angel of my heaven" (83). Against the submerged and subterranean dark-god aspect of Dionys, Basil is all transcendence and white light, and would have Daphne be the same. During this conversation, the Count sits in his dark blue uniform, his "dark flame of life" seeming to "glow through the cloth from his body" (84). By contrast, a "curious white passion" glows from Basil's face as they talk. It is significant that Dionys's dark glow comes from his body, Basil's light one from his head. Basil has told Dionys that the war's good side is that man will arrive "at a higher state of consciousness, and therefore of life. And so, of course, a higher plane of love" (84). Basil's

---

brothers, *remain faithful to the earth"* (125). The way to becoming the overman is by going under: "I love those who do not know how to live, except by going under, for they are those who cross over" (127). Were there space, this thought would have made an excellent motto for Dionys's thimble. Zarathustra's mascots, incidentally, emblematizing the over-under aspect of his ethic, are an eagle and a *snake*. To do justice to all the analogies really would require a separate chapter.

insistence upon higher consciousness against Dionys's championing of the subconscious is simply a vertical rendering of what all along has been the inner-versus-outer polarity of the story. In a later passage that contains the germ of a novel to come, Daphne reflects upon the opposition in a way that conflates once again each category of metaphor:

> It was her one passion at Thoresway to hear the dependents talk and talk—about everything. The curious feeling of intimacy across a breach fascinated her. Their lives fascinated her: what they thought, what they *felt*. These, what they felt. That fascinated her. There was a gamekeeper she could have loved—an impudent, ruddy-faced, laughing, ingratiating fellow; she could have loved him, if he had not been isolated beyond the breach of his birth, her culture, her consciousness. Her *consciousness* seemed to make a great gulf between her and the lower classes, the unconscious classes. She accepted it as her doom. She could never meet in real contact anyone but a super-conscious, finished being like herself: or like her husband. Her father had some of the unconscious blood-warmth of the lower classes. But he was like a man who is damned. And the Count, of course. The Count had something that was hot and invisible, a dark flame of life that might warm the cold white fire of her own blood. (98–99)

Lawrence here not only states the conflict in the familiar terms, he establishes also a further dimension, that of class—in terms once again of higher and lower.

The specific manifestation of Basil's higher consciousness is law; by contrast, the expression of Dionys's instinctual under-self is power. Since most discussions of *The Ladybird* center upon Dionys's elaboration of his "natural aristocracy" with its watchwords of "power" and "submission," there is not much need to lay out the conversation between Dionys and Basil on the subject. The discussion is certainly not extraneous to the central action. Whatever the merits of the ideas, it parallels and reinforces Daphne's later submission at Thoresway to Dionys. Moreover, it leads naturally into a further development that is of utmost importance to the story: Dionys's elaboration of the meaning of the ladybird. Dionys's aristocracy is based upon the relationship between master and subject of earlier ages. Asked by Basil about the emblem while they are at Thoresway, Dionys says that it has a long genealogy: "It is a descendant of the Egyptian scarabeus, which is a very mysterious emblem. So I connect myself with the Pharoahs: just through my ladybird" (96). Daphne then remarks upon the "ages" through which it has "crept," and Lord Beveridge quotes Fabre on the insect: "He suggests that the beetle rolling a little ball of dung before him, in a dry old field, must have suggested to the Egyptians the First Principle that set the globe rolling." Basil says, "That the earth is a tiny ball of dry dung is good," and Lady Beveridge observes, "That is what it is, to go back to one's origins." Dionys then follows up: "Perhaps they meant that it was the principle of decomposition which first set the ball rolling" (97). Lawrence's giving each character a voice in the explication is interesting because each in a sense becomes implicated. The discussion also catches up two earlier developments: first, it projects Dionys's destroyer role, announced earlier, as a primal and necessary one (the "red hammer" is *original*, a "first Principle"); and second, it takes the central metaphor into the dimension of time. The process of going inward, rediscovering the knowledge that all the while has been within the blood, also traces a return along a temporal dimension to an age before such knowledge was repressed. Appropriate, then, is the fact that Dionys has an "aboriginal little face" (45).

It is the mysticism of the last ten pages or so of the story that most annoys the story's critics. They fail to recognize, however, that the embodiment of the action in terms of myth is precisely along the lines of development the imagery has been tracing. The myth here not only encompasses almost all of this imagery, but also, in the coming together of Dionys and Daphne through their marriage in darkness, might be said to climax this imagery. The presiding myth of the ancient Eleusinian mysteries is enacted in these last pages. Lawrence strategically returns us to the source, inward and downward in time and space, out of the light of the present into the dark of the aboriginal past. Though neither Dis (Pluto) nor Persephone is called by name, clearly their story is acted out here. To drape the central action with a religious mantle is simply to confirm further the sanctity of the heart's—the blood's—affections.

In short, the ending replicates the action, if not quite the poetic magnificence, of "Bavarian Gentians," which after all is as much about life ("the living dark") as about death. At Thoresway, Daphne finds that she cannot sleep at night. She was "like a neurotic, . . . nailed inside her own fretful self-consciousness." She hears Dionys singing softly in his room, a "small, bat-like sound," like one "alone in his own blood" (99–100). The singing at first has the effect of transporting "her upper spirit" beyond "the world . . . where her soul balanced like a bird on wings, and was perfected":

> So it was, in her upper spirit. But underneath was a wild, wild yearning, actually to go, actually to be given. Actually to go, actually to die the death, actually to cross the border and be gone, to be gone. To be gone from this herself, from this Daphne, to be gone from father and mother, brothers and husband, and home and land and world: to be gone. To be gone to the call from the beyond: the call! It was the Count calling. He was calling her. She was sure he was calling her. Out of herself, out of her world, he was calling her. (100–101).

On the third night, she goes as far as the oak armchair outside his room. At last the singing stops, and his light goes out. But it starts again, "the most terrible song of all. It began with a rather dreary, slow horrible sound, like death." Then came "the real call, . . . most imperative, and utterly inhuman" (101–2). The details—"upper spirit," "die the death," "inhuman"— are all in accord with the story's imagery and the myth now beginning to take shape. Inside, the room is "complete darkness" with "no moon outside." Their two presences are the "darkness answering to darkness, and deep answering to deep." They sit beside one another, and "the darkness inside the room seemed alive like blood" (102–3). When they touch, he thinks that he has "no future in this life," though "the after-life belonged to him." Although he first thinks it best to proceed alone, he changes his mind: "No, no. The next life was his. He was master of the after-life. Why fear for this life? Why not take the soul she offered him? Now and for ever, for the life that would come when they both were dead. Take her into the underworld. Take her into the dark Hades with him, like Francesca and Paolo. And in hell hold her fast, queen of the underworld, himself master of the underworld" (104). He tells her that he has no power in the day, but that "In the night, in the dark, and in death, you are mine" (104). The myth as Lawrence renders it has, of course, no mourning Ceres, though either Lady Beveridge or Basil could fill the role. Basil in fact now regards Daphne as a "sister," with "all the sex and the desire gone" (106). But no mourning Ceres is required. What Lawrence chiefly requires is an immediate context. The Dis-Persephone myth resonates with almost all the story's developments and details. It both absorbs and projects the external-internal duality. Some days later, for instance, when Daphne considers what her life will be after Dionys leaves, she does so in a figure that places an inside within an inside: "No, she had found this wonderful thing after she had heard him singing: she had suddenly collapsed away from her old self into this darkness, this peace, this quiescence that was like a full dark river flowing eternally in her soul" (107). And then comes a figure that doubles ingeniously upon itself, picking up still another strand of the story's interconnecting imagery: "She had gone to sleep from the *nuit blanche* of her days." That is, the "ravishment" has laid to rest Basil's white, self-conscious "moon-mother of the world" (77), his Aphrodite-of-the-foam Daphne ("actually to die the death . . . , to be gone from this herself, from this Daphne"), and revived the aboriginal, primal self, the Queen-of-the-Underworld Daphne. The added temporal dimension of the story, as provided by the myth, allows us to see more clearly the way that the central action of Lawrence's fiction supports (with its peculiar Lawrencian implications, to be sure) Eliot's famous observation that the end of "exploration" is to arrive where one began "and know the place for the first time." Daphne's (re)discovery of her unconscious self is really a return—a coming back *in*, after a going *out*.

Earlier I used the word "conceit" to describe the organization of metaphor in *The Ladybird*. And I referred to the metaphors themselves as being "organic" and "enabling." They are organic in the obvious sense: the details, leaf and branch, are of the same sap as the tree—synecdochically, they each contain the whole or at least suggest the possibility of it. Just as the Hades myth enacts the central action and meaning, so the imagery implies the myth: the lily, for instance, with its white, but cold beauty in the upper world, its dark, vital roots in the underworld. They are organic further in the way they almost never are merely local. They are not only connected with the trunk, so to speak, but throughout are *in relation to each other*, as I have shown. Dionys, to take just one further instance, refers to Daphne's beauty as her "whited sepulchre" (67). It is hardly necessary to explain how this detail, which anticipates the lily figure by a number of pages, not only contains embryonically the central meaning, but also enables the lily image, in its relations to the whole, to expand its implications. This is Lawrence's technique throughout the story: to allow one image to enable another image so that together they organically comprehend the whole. This is not to say that *The Ladybird* is Lawrence's masterpiece among his five or six short novels. I do believe, however, that understanding how he has dramatized inwardness and outwardness through metaphor gives us a keener appreciation both of the story itself and of the direction taken by his subsequent longer fictions. It also indicates why Lawrence might have felt that *The Ladybird* possessed "the quick of a new thing."

Chapter 4

Of Bits, Beasts, and Bush
The Interior Wilderness in *Kangaroo*

The "quickness" of *The Ladybird* lay in Lawrence's creation through metaphor of a subtext that was largely absent from the two companion novellas. To a lesser or greater degree, a novel lives by its imagery. For some novels, the imagery provides the texture or shading that argues significance for the action; it is the context or subcontext within which the events of the novel come to mean. The later novels of D. H. Lawrence are chiefly of this sort. The slightest, though hardly the shortest, of the novels of Lawrence's maturity is *The Lost Girl*, which scrapes by with the least imagery of his longer works—and is resultantly thin. On the other hand, *The Plumed Serpent*, the novel most freighted with imagery, is his largest failure, in large part because the imagery (chiefly symbolic) fails to suggest very much beyond obvious correspondences. The symbols become reductive, creating a drag upon the action. To be sure, a thinness of characterization also attends the failures of these novels. *The Lost Girl* suffers decidedly because the reader, on the basis of what he has been shown of Ciccio, has difficulty crediting Alvina's submissive love for him. Similarly, in *The Plumed Serpent*, Ramón and Cipriano do not convince us as gurus of the New Religion because they do not convince us as characters. One can argue that in *Kangaroo* Lawrence could have ascribed less of himself to Somers and created more of a fictional character, but it is precisely because the author enters his own doubts and uncertainties, in sometimes bewildering profusion, that Somers is an immeasurably better "creation" than either Don Ramón or Don Cipriano.

Conversely, *Lady Chatterley's Lover* succeeds, through the first two-thirds of it at least, because the imagery of sex and nature creates a larger world for us (we might almost say distracting us from the "Lawrenceness" of Mellors). To the extent that his fiction achieves this amplification, Lawrence is one of the outstanding imaginers of twentieth-century fiction, the suggestiveness of his imagery perhaps as powerful as any author's since Melville. Nor is it inappropriate to mention Melville in this regard, for *Kangaroo* is Lawrence's *Moby-Dick*. One would not want to press this point in very many particulars, but in the apparent discursiveness of its form and movement and in the largeness and suggestive power of its symbols, it has striking similarities with the novel Lawrence expressed fascination for in *Studies in Classic American Literature*, published like *Kangaroo* in 1923 though written before it. The reader of *Kangaroo* does not travel in seas so vast and deep as those of *Moby-Dick*; nonetheless, *Kangaroo* is the most narratively impressive and artistically successful novel of Lawrence's last decade.

Next to *The Plumed Serpent*, however, *Kangaroo* is probably Lawrence's most thoroughly disliked novel. For John Middleton Murry, in spite of the beauty of some descriptive passages, *Kangaroo* remains "a chaotic book," largely because of the "internal chaos" of Somers-Lawrence, who is no longer a character but merely the "fragments" of one. Eliseo Vivas finds the book to be largely "padding" and dismisses Graham Hough's contention that the seemingly digressive sections are actually a part of "an authentic process of living growth." Vivas argues that since Lawrence (as Somers) clearly was *not* growing at the time of the novel's action, we may thereby disqualify any claim for the relevance of these sections. Julian Moynahan believes the work to be "the most padded and redundant of Lawrence's novels," from "a formal point of view . . . a heap of bits and fragments"; he concludes that "the consequences of [Somers-Lawrence's] self-indulgence, from the standpoints of intelligence, sincerity, and humanity, are such as would make an angel weep." For Keith Sagar, the novel merely "flounders on," Lawrence having lost interest in it early.[1]

Such criticism represents the consensus about the novel. But there is dissent from a minority. I mention above, for instance, Graham Hough's maverick opinion. More recently John Worthen has argued that the novel is one of Lawrence's more deliberate works, that the narrative chattiness is "an attempt to be honest and clear and truthful beyond the limits of . . . self-consciousness and . . . moralising," and that the reader should view the work in the context of essays about the novel and its form that Lawrence wrote at about this time. In *Kangaroo*, Somers (by way of Harriet) says that "life doesn't start with a form. It starts with a new feeling, and ends with a form" (111). Worthen argues persuasively that Lawrence's explorations in *Kangaroo* into so many different areas—sociology, economics, psychology, religion—reflect not an amateurism, but "the novel's insistence that modern man necessarily lives through such involvements— through, indeed, such very fragmentariness."[2] Whether discussions like Worthen's will sway many skeptics is doubtful because the novel is *sui generis*—so out of the mainstream that "taste" may more often than not be

    1. Murry, *D. H. Lawrence: Son of Woman*, 238–39; Vivas, *D. H. Lawrence: The Failure and the Triumph of Art*, 37–38; Hough, *The Dark Sun: A Study of D. H. Lawrence*, 106; Moynahan, *The Deed of Life: The Novels and Tales of D. H. Lawrence*, 101–2, 105; Sagar, *The Art of D. H. Lawrence*, 136.
    2. John Worthen, *D. H. Lawrence and the Idea of the Novel*, 142–43.

the arbiter. But one would like to think that readers will begin to take the book more seriously in its artistic aspect. In the ways that Worthen speaks of and in Lawrence's quite deliberate, and I think successful, architecture of symbol and symbolic detail to undergird meaning, *Kangaroo* is a formidable and compelling novel. The symbolic detail is the subject of this chapter. That the imagery has not been considered important, nor even much noticed for that matter, is symptomatic of the general underestimation of Lawrence's achievement here. The imagery is essential to conveying the magnitude and complexity of the central symbol, the bush. The Australian bush, is an immense and omnipresent symbol governing nearly every development of the novel, which is Lawrence's "wilderness" book.

I

Fairly early in the action (chapter 4), Harriet wonders aloud why she and Somers cannot stay on in Australia: "And why couldn't we be happy in this wonderful new country, living to ourselves. We could have a cow, and chickens—and then the Pacific." She says that surely these are enough for any man. Why should Somers want more? He replies, "Because I feel I *must* fight out something with mankind yet. I haven't finished with my fellow man" (77). Almost three hundred pages later, in the last chapter, having fought out battles with Kangaroo and Jack and with Willie Struthers, he finds himself responding in almost the same way when Jaz urges him to remain in Sydney. He tells Jaz that if he did stay it would be to live in the bush. But he will not give in yet.

> "And another thing," said Richard. "I won't give up the flag of our real civilized consciousness. I'll give up the ideals. But not the aware, self-responsible, deep consciousness that we've gained. I won't go back on that, Jaz, though Kangaroo did say I was the enemy of civilization."
> "You don't consider you are, then?" asked Jaz, pertinently.
> "The enemy of civilization? Well, I'm the enemy of this machine civilization and this ideal civilization. But I'm not the enemy of the deep, self-responsible consciousness in man, which is what *I* mean by civilization. In that sense of civilization I'd fight forever for the flag and try to carry it on into deeper, darker places. It's an adventure, Jaz, like any other. And when you realize what you're doing, it's perhaps the best adventure." (383)

For "machine civilization" we might read Willie Struthers'; for "ideal civilization," Kangaroo's. The "deeper, darker places" are, of course, those in the bush. But the lack of people in the bush means that Somers, who would be attracted to uninhabited wilderness if he did not still have a fight on his hands, is not disposed to stay. The novel indeed has been an "adventure," even with all the quotidian oddments that numerous critics have found distracting and irrelevant. But we must remember that this is a novel about a man who has struggled with belief, who has been through a "nightmare," yet must live in the daily round of "bits" of things here and there. It is through an understanding of what Lawrence has in mind for these "bits" that one arrives at a sense of the largeness of this novel's conception.

That something may be afoot in a strategic sense might be apparent from the title of chapter 14: "Bits." "Bits" is a column in the *Sydney Bulletin* consisting of unrelated short items that Somers rather likes: "Bits, bits, bits. Yet Richard Lovat read on. It was not mere anecdotage. It was the sheer momentaneous life of the continent. There was no consecutive thread. Only the laconic courage of experience" (300). *Kangaroo* might seem to be the same, having no "consecutive thread." Somers's life, fallen into disorganization as a result of the war, seems also to have no consecutive thread; he has only his sense of "the dark God" at the heart of himself. The narrative, fragmented as it is, reflects and reinforces Somers's condition. But at the center of this novel is also a unity, a dark god of its own, the bush. The surface, though, is bits. In chapter 1, Lawrence describes the neighborhood surrounding Torestin, the bungalow Somers and Harriet have rented: "This was one of the old-fashioned bits of Sydney" (17). The houses are "little dog-kennels" or "chicken houses." Tin cans lie scattered about. Sydney did not "seem to be real, it seemed to be sprinkled on the surface of a darkness into which it never penetrated" (18). The image is significant. What passes for civilization rims the country, all on the outside, the surface. The real civilization is within, in the interior: "But the bush, the grey, charred bush. It scared him. . . . Waiting, waiting—the bush seemed to be horribly waiting. And he couldn't penetrate into its secret" (18–19). But this novel is, as Somers thinks of it in the "Bits" chapter, a "thought-adventure" (308) into its secret—or toward it, for the nature of Somers's "Lord God Almighty" is not to be known or seen. But first the "bits" must be left behind, the surface must be penetrated, for the secret even to be approached.

How important these *bits* are to the structure of the book is evident from the sheer incidence of the word. "Bit" or "bits" appears in *every* chapter of the novel. Often it occurs on the first page or two of a chapter, as if Lawrence, having designed its presence in each chapter, wished to secure its use early. Even if he did not have such a design, the frequency of the word simply indicates how deeply the structure of the novel comes from within Lawrence. For as I have indicated, like *The Ladybird* (indeed, if less insistently, like most of Lawrence's fiction), *Kangaroo* is about outsides and insides. In Lawrence's view, civilization or humanity is mainly "outside" now, all surface, when it should be "inside," and visible when it should be invisible. James Trewhella (Jaz) cautions Harriet about Somers's involvement in Australian political matters, telling her that the diggers will drag Somers down to their level. Jaz can say this because, being Cornish, he is at the same time of them and not of them: "I've got another set of eyes inside me somewhere that can tell real differences, when there are any. And that's what these people don't seem to have at all. They've only got the outside eyes" (82–83).[3] When Victoria Callcott implicitly offers herself to Somers, he resists on the basis that for her it is purely a "visual," outside thing: "These moments bred in the head and born in the eye: he had enough of them. These flashes of desire for a visual object would no longer carry him into action. . . . There was a downslope into Orcus, and a vast, phallic, sacred darkness. . . . He would meet there or nowhere" (160). Australia, the land, embodies almost precisely what Somers means here: "The strange, as it were, *invisible* beauty of Australia . . . which seems to lurk just beyond the range of our white vision. You feel you can't *see*—as if your eyes hadn't the vision in them to correspond with the outside landscape" (87).

Australia, then, with its narrow coastal veneer of "civilization" and its immense, uncharted, dark interior is an almost perfect objective correlative for the outer and inner human worlds that Lawrence wishes to investigate. The shabby bungalows with their rats (which infest both Torestin and Coo-ee) and tin cans symbolize the disorganized, fragmented, mental ("outside") world of all-too-human humanity. The corrective to this condition lies within, but it is a primitive, frightening interior, a wilderness, dangerous and difficult of access. The human "bits," fearing this interior self or world, live on the outside. When Lawrence does not describe them through analogy as rats, then they are "ants" or "hollow stalks." He has Kangaroo speak of them as "ant-men" and "ant-women" (135–36). Since Somers has much the same attitude, he is drawn to Kangaroo at this early point in their relationship (and will continue in a sense to be). Both men believe that people should be "happy . . . unconsciously, rather than unhappy consciously" (134). At later meetings, however, their differences become apparent. For one thing, Somers's notion of the unconscious is different from Kangaroo's. For another, they are finally quite at odds in their views of humanity. Kangaroo, for all his earlier disgust toward people as ants, now speaks of them generously and forgivingly. Somers will have none of it.

3. Harry T. Moore (*The Priest of Love*, 349) errs in equating Jaz with "the cunning, evil Cornishmen" of Lawrence's 1917 experience. Jaz in fact, though a Cornishman, embodies on occasion the "dark" qualities that Somers admires. Jack, on the other hand, though an Australian, more nearly represents the mean-spiritedness that Moore has in mind.

Describing them within the configurations of the inside-outside trope, he says the Australians are "marvelous and manly and independent and all that, outside. But inside, they are not. When they're *quite* alone, they don't exist." They lack "the last everlasting central bit of soul, solitary soul, that makes a man himself. They all merge to the outside, away from the center" (146–47).

Thus, they shy from the vast solitary center of Australia, the bush, and take up their fragmented existences at the safe perimeter. By relinquishing that "bit" of solitary soul, they become all "bits." In chapter 12, "The Nightmare," Lawrence describes the exacted price of this loss:

> And there *is* this bitter and sordid after-war price to pay because men lost their heads, and worse, lost their inward, individual integrity. And when a man loses his inward, isolated, manly integrity, it is a bad day for that man's true wife. A true man should not lose his head. The greater the crisis, the more intense should be his isolated reckoning with his own soul. And *then* let him act, of his own whole self. Not fling himself away: or much worse, let himself be *dragged* away, bit by bit. (236–37)

A man should not "be *dragged* away, bit by bit" until the "isolate and absolute individual self" disintegrates and "all is relative." Relativity is one of Lawrence's devils in *Kangaroo* (though Somers's "devil" is also part of his god) except when it becomes "relative to the absolute" (309). But this condition seldom obtains: "The people of this terrestrial sphere are all bits. Isolate one of them, and he is still only a bit. Isolate your man in the street, and he is just a rudimentary fragment" (309–10). This passage helps explain Lawrence-Somers's insistence upon obedience to the dark interior god at the same time that he insists upon man's duty to the social world outside:

> That is the beginning and end, the alpha and the omega, the one absolute: the man alone by himself, alone with his own soul, alone with his eyes on the darkness which is the dark god of life. Alone like a pythoness on her tripod, like the oracle alone above the fissure into the unknown. The oracle, the fissure down into the unknown, the strange exhalations from the dark, the strange words that the oracle must utter. Strange cruel, pregnant words: the new term of consciousness.
>
> This is the innermost symbol of man: alone in the darkness of the cavern of himself, listening to soundlessness of inflowing fate. Inflowing fate, inflowing doom, what does it matter? The man by himself—that is the absolute—listening—that is the relativity—for the influx of his fate, or doom. (310)

The passage indicates how Lawrence can have Somers say he will not give up the "flag of our real civilized consciousness" (the man listening at the fissure) yet simultaneously offer devotionals to the unconscious self (the oracle speaking from her seat within the "unknown"). The problem is that men do not listen anymore: they are "deaf and dumb scurrying ants . . . fallen out of living relativity" (311). It is not strictly necessary then that mankind inhabit the bush, the interior wilderness, but mankind had better heed the exhalations of the oracle—or devil or beast—and its "strange, cruel . . . new term of consciousness."

II

Vivas attacks Lawrence's inclusion of the newspaper excerpts in "Volcanic Evidence" as padding. He argues that in a novel about Lawrence-Somers's growth the quotation of a scientific article is superfluous because "neither Somers nor Lawrence was dedicated to growth through the acquisition of knowledge."[4] However that may be, the statement ignores or misses the sort of internal logic that Lawrence has taken some pains to establish through analogy and symbol. The outside-inside opposition, for instance, works here and it works in connection with another category of imagery, that of demon and beast. The former is the more frequent and the more important, but the beast (in the wild) also enriches (and helps to create) Lawrence's meanings. The misreading—if that is the right word— by Vivas, one of Lawrence's more interesting and responsible critics, is symptomatic of the treatment *Kangaroo* has received. Because the outer layer of the book can appear to be a refuse-heap of Lawrence's random philosophizing, readers do not think to look for an inside, where I believe we find a vital bush with strongly rich—and coherent—exhalations. It took us almost a hundred years to see that, finally, almost nothing in *Moby-Dick* is extraneous. And, as I have said, *Kangaroo* bears a resemblance in technique to *Moby-Dick*.

On Somers's first meeting with Kangaroo, Kangaroo quotes him the first lines of Blake's poem: "Tyger, tyger, burning bright / In the forests of the night." He asks Somers, "The lion of your might would be a tiger, wouldn't it? The tiger and the unicorn were fighting for the crown" (128). Lawrence, of course, is having Kangaroo restate the symbols for the opposing principles of "The Crown." Somers asks if the tiger is Kangaroo's "principle of evil." Kangaroo replies, "No, no. The tiger stands on one side of the shield, and the unicorn on the other, and they don't fight for the crown at all. They keep it between them. The pillars of the world! The tiger and the

4. Vivas, *Failure and Triumph*, 37–38.

kangaroo!" (128). Thus, Lawrence reconstitutes the 1915 essay to accommodate the dimensions of this novel. The important thing to notice, however, is the way that "The Tyger" lines look forward to "Volcanic Evidence" (chapter 7) and "'Revenge!' Timotheus Cries" (chapter 13) with the image of the volcano and bright lava about to erupt from within. The tiger in the forest or the beast in the bush symbolizes the Lawrence ethic. Somers has told Kangaroo that Somers's god enters "not through the spirit" but "from the lower self, the dark self, the phallic self" (150). Kangaroo chooses to think of this god as a "demon" that he is going to "exorcise" (151), thus giving the lie to his earlier statement that the tiger is not his principle of evil: "I can see that there is a beast in the way. There is a beast in your eyes, Lovat." He tells Somers further, "You hurt me with the demon that is in you" (151).

The reader may see, then, the consistency of Lawrence's images: the tiger in the forests of the night, the lava in the volcano, the "devil in [Somers's] belly" (183). The imagery reinforces both the Australia-bush, outwardness-inwardness figure and the Lawrence phallic ethic. References abound to Somers as a "serpent," an "adder," a "viper." What Lawrence has in mind, almost certainly, is a revaluation such as Blake posits in "The Tyger." Thus, "the one dark God, the Unknown," is "a hell-god" (314). The more the reader contemplates the apocalyptic undersurface of *Kangaroo*, the clearer it becomes that this novel derives from the start made with *The Ladybird* and leads toward *The Plumed Serpent*, the distinctly inferior novel of the two, and how *Kangaroo* is itself some rough beast slouching toward Mexico. In "Volcanic Evidence," Somers worries over the problems that develop between Harriet and himself when he listens too long and too closely to his dark god:

> What does she want? She won't leave a fellow alone. I felt fairly beatific last evening—I felt I could swim Australia into a future, and that Jaz was wonderful, and I was a sort of central angel. So now I must admit I am flabbergasted at finding my devil coiled up exultant like a black cat in my belly this morning, purring all the more loudly because of my 'goodness' of last evening, and lashing his tail so venomously at the sight of the two women in the black 'costumes'. Is this devil after all my god? Do I stand with the debbil-debbil worshippers, in spite of all my efforts and protestations? (184)

Lawrence-Somers is not yet ready to say yes. Lawrence-Cipriano will be, in spite of Kate Leslie's sometime protestations. But Lawrence-Somers is close: "Well, all right then, if I *am* finally a sort of human bomb, black inside, and primed; I hope the hour and place will come for my going off." He concludes that "*some* men have to be bombs, to explode and make breaches in the walls that shut life in" (184). The metaphor instances once more the imagery of internal force or energy present throughout *Kangaroo*. The passage appropriately brings Lawrence to the excerpted article on volcanoes from the Sydney *Daily Telegraph* on "Sleeping Volcanoes." Along the entire east coast of Australia, the article says, there is today neither live nor dead volcano, though there exists "basaltic evidence" of ancient volcanic action. Yet "we know nothing whatever of the awful forces at work beneath the crust of the earth, and nothing of the internal fires, or that awful subterranean abode where Shelley said 'the old earthquake Demon nurses her young Ruin'" (187). Somers reads, as we can imagine Lawrence did, "with satisfaction" this account of volcanic evidence. The conflation of volcanoes and hell serves the narrative perfectly. Somers thinks, "If the mother earth herself is so unstable, and upsets the apple-cart without caring a straw, why, what can a man say to himself if he *does* happen to have a devil in his belly" (187). Daniel J. Schneider rightly discusses the volcano in relation to Somers's conflict between "sympathetic connection" with the world of men and politics on the one hand, and on the other a "voluntary resistance [to] and rejection" of the social world.[5] The volcano is the objective correlative of Somers's "devilishness" that opposes social immersion. He recognizes that "before mankind would accept any man for a king, and before Harriet would ever accept him, Richard Lovat, as a lord and master, he . . . must open the doors of his soul and let in a dark Lord and Master of himself." Once he lets in "this fearful god" who "enters us from below," the rest "would happen" (196). Somers is merely continuing the course of action that Count Johann Dionys Psanek began.

Chapter 13, "'Revenge!' Timotheus Cries," builds upon "The Nightmare." In it Lawrence picks up again the imagery of "Volcanic Evidence." Somers realizes that since 1918 fury and fear have lain "deep in his unconsciousness . . . like frenzied lava" (287). Critics have charged Lawrence-Somers with coming to rest in "internal chaos," with "moral bankruptcy," with being one whose only discovery is that of "the meaninglessness of meaning."[6] The mood of this chapter is angry and violent—it portrays Somers in one of his darkest moments. But if readers pay attention to the imagery they will see that the whole thrust of Somers's effort is toward hopefulness and life—out of a condition of surface despair. Without moving away from the structure of his controlling imagery, he now gives over the tactical imagery of devils and lava. The focus remains on the conscious (outer) and the unconscious (inner): "For he believed in the inward soul, in

5. Schneider, "Psychology and Art in Lawrence's *Kangaroo*," 163–65.
6. Murry, *Son of Woman*, 238; Moynahan, *Deed of Life*, 106; Sagar, *Art of Lawrence*, 136.

the profound unconscious of man. Not an ideal God. The ideal God is a proposition of the mental consciousness, all-too-limitedly-human" (294). But now he introduces images of well and womb, of water and birth—in short, of life:

> And every *living* human soul is a well-head to this darkness of the living unutterable. Into every living soul wells up the darkness, the unutterable. And then there is travail of the visible with the invisible. Man is in travail with his own soul, while ever his soul lives. Into his unconscious surges a new flood of the God-darkness, the living unutterable. . . . And this unutterable is like a germ, a foetus with which he must travail, bring it at last into utterance, into action, into *being*. . . . The long travail. The long gestation of the soul within a man, and the final parturition, the birth of a new way of knowing, a new God-influx. A new idea, true enough. But at the centre, the old anti-idea: the dark, the unutterable God. This time not a God scribbling on tablets of stone or bronze. No everlasting decalogues. No sermons on mounts, either. The dark God, the forever unrevealed. (294–95)

Although five chapters remain in the book, this one marks the resolution of this particular development of the imagery. It rests, however, within the womb of an image much larger (in both meanings of the word), extending from first chapter to last, from west to east coast: the bush.

III

What is this "bush" and what is Lawrence's strategy concerning it? The reader may perceive this novel, at least at first, the way that Lawrence initially saw *Moby-Dick*: "At first you are put off by the style. It reads like journalism. It seems spurious. You feel Melville is trying to put something over on you. It won't do." About Moby Dick himself Lawrence wrote:

> Of course he is a symbol.
> Of what?
> I doubt if even Melville knew exactly. That's the best of it. (*Studies in Classic American Literature*, 145)

Lawrence, however, has a better notion of what his central symbol signifies than he suspects Melville has of his. Lawrence's reading of *Moby-Dick*, I suggested earlier, influenced his writing of *Kangaroo*. Here is the same journalistic style, development through digressions (especially evidenced by "The Nightmare" chapter), inclusion of writing from other sources, heavy philosophical freight, and a large, seemingly unwieldy symbol. The wilderness here is not the ocean (though the ocean is a tremendous presence in *Kangaroo*, sandwiching, with the bush, the fragile little layer of civilization), but the vast interior of the continent. The similarities extend even to the narrators: both are isolates, both metaphysical voyagers. At the end of "The Nightmare," Somers feels "broken off from his fellow men, his ties broken: *He was loose like a single timber of some wrecked ship, drifting over the face of the earth. Without a people, without a land. So be it. He was broken apart, apart he would remain*" (287; my italics). It would also be easy to point up similarities in Ishmael's and Somers's distrust of such things as the abstractions of the "spirit." We recall Ishmael's admonition to the masthead dreamer adrift on the perilous mental seas of "Pantheism." But the main likeness is apparent in Lawrence's appropriation of the kind of symbol he believed to be at the heart of *Moby-Dick*: a wilderness symbol, deliberately vague, and above all mysterious. When Lawrence writes in *Studies in Classic American Literature* that Moby Dick "is the deepest blood-being of the white race; he is our deepest blood-nature" and that he is "hunted into the death of upper consciousness and the ideal will. Our blood-self subjected to our will" (160), he is writing of the condition that frets Somers throughout *Kangaroo*. The bush is the aboriginal, mysterious symbol of our "unconscious," "blood" self. In *Moby-Dick*, as Lawrence perceives the novel, this self is hunted down; in *Kangaroo*, it is fled from. In either instance, man's conscious loathing and fear of the unconscious, instinctual self drives him.

To be sure, the fact that Lawrence apparently was influenced by *Moby-Dick* does not make *Kangaroo* itself a better novel. What matters is the coherence of the symbols, or images, their resonance with character and plot, and their organic indivisibility with the action and meaning. *Kangaroo* is a novel about advocacies. Kangaroo the character is an advocate for a spiritual love between a patriarchal leader and his followers; Willie Struthers is an advocate for the comradely love between "mates"; Harriet is the advocate for conjugal love, with its implications of possession and merging. Somers finds himself variously attracted and repelled by these advocacies, which, whatever his inclination at the moment, do not leave off pulling at him. His own advocacy we know very well. It is as these several advocacies are set into relief, ascribed dimension against the background of Australia and its bush, that they move from comparative abstraction to comparative concreteness and immediacy. Without, in other words, what critics have often called its "travel book" aspect, particularly that aspect involving the bush and the associative imagery Lawrence is able to work off of it, *Kangaroo* would be extremely thin broth, much as *The Lost Girl* is. Instead, therefore, of complaining that this thing gets in the way of that thing in the novel or that this thing is merely flourish and irrelevancy, one might attempt to see what a writer conscious of his craft would be trying to do with "this" or with "that." Lawrence has his faults, to be sure, among them his tendency in some novels to write all-too-thinly disguised autobiography and his tendency to repeat himself. Neither of these, however, should obscure the fact that Lawrence very often has a method. That this method is not always at the surface may be its virtue, not its weakness.

For instance, Somers has a beard—as does Lawrence. Twice this beard is mentioned on the first page. The lunching workmen observe Somers, "a smallish man, pale-faced, with a dark beard," who is also described as the "strange, foreign-looking little man with the beard" (13). Thus the details would appear to be both autobiographical and repetitive. But is that all that they are? In "The Nightmare," the beard figures again. Somers is threatened, should he be conscripted, with having his beard shaved: "He said in his heart, the day his beard was shaven he was beaten, lost. He identified it with his isolate manhood" (238). Later, when he is called for his examination, the same threat arises: "Oh, yes, they intended to make him feel they had got their knife into him. They would have his beard off, too!" (283). Afterwards he thinks: "They wanted to set their foot absolutely on life, grind it down, and be masters. Masters, as they were of the foul machine. . . . Masters of money-power, with an obscene hatred of life, true spontaneous life" (284). It is not difficult to make a connection between those who wish to shave off Somers's beard with those who wish to destroy the White Whale. As enemies of the "true, spontaneous life," they must exist within "the death of upper consciousness and the ideal will." But why, the reader may ask, do they regard the beard as inimical to their "white mental consciousness"?

The answer, of course, is that the beard is emblem for the "dark," "isolate," "unconscious" self—that is, it is a synecdoche for the novel's central symbol, the bush. When Victoria Callcott first meets Somers, it is his beard and green coat, significantly, that make an impression upon her. We are told a few pages later that she is "fascinated by him: she of course imagined some sort of God in the fiery bush." Jack is not so impressed: "If there was an individual inside the brightly burning bush . . . , even if it was a sort of God in the bush, let him come out, man to man" (45). Jack, who reveals himself in the end to be like the Cornishmen who want Somers's beard, is wary of Somers's god. Being an individual who lives outwardly, he distrusts and has no use for the inward self. In wearing green, Somers anticipates Oliver Mellors, a more fully developed Green Man. Somers's beard and the green coat conflate to form *bush*. Interesting also is that when Jack first sees his new neighbors at Torestin they are staring at him through a thin place in the "dark green" bush that forms a hedge between their two bungalows. The fact that it is "weary" looking and has "dead" places catches up similar aspects of the greater bush, with its pallid, dead trees from the burning off.

Part of the reader's problem is that the bush, in its aboriginal aspect, is not the same thing all the time; that is to say, Lawrence does not commit consistency upon his symbol. It has different colorations and produces different effects. In chapter 10, "The Diggers" chapter midway through the novel, Lawrence uses the "fern-world" aspect of the bush to describe a lethargy affecting all the characters at this point. Harriet (she and Somers have had their big fight) feels herself loving Richard rather quiveringly, "and yet in the quiver of her passion was some of this indifference, this twilight indifference of the fern-world." Somers too "drifts away into the grey pre-world where men . . . didn't have emotions and personal consciousness, but were shadowy like trees, and on the whole silent, with numb brains and slow limbs and a great indifference" (198). Similarly, when Jack and Victoria come for the weekend, he sits apathetically: "The aboriginal *sympathetic* apathy was upon him, he was like some creature that has lost its soul" (202). Certainly this drifting tendency against making "any effort to consciousness whatsoever" (203) is not one the book approves. The use of the word "consciousness" gives us the clue, however, as to how to deal with Lawrence's rendering of the bush and the "aboriginal" here. Though we can make the case usually in Lawrence, we must not expect consciousness in all its manifestations to be always bad, as we must not expect unconsciousness in all its manifestations to be always good. One does, however, receive life at its source, which for Lawrence is always the unconscious. So he must listen there from time to time if he is to achieve a fully self-responsible consciousness. Thus, the beard that this man who contends for "our real civilized consciousness" wears is at the same time the emblem of the dark unconscious world, the realm of the "fearful god," the bush. Somers's "manhood," his "individuality," is organized in the unconscious self and leads to his "real civilized consciousness," which contains this unconscious self.

As the bush is presented at the beginning, it is an equivocal symbol. The attendant imagery is more repellent than otherwise. The bush is "so dark, like grey-green iron. And then it was so deathly still." It "seemed to be hoarily waiting," harboring a secret "he could not penetrate" (18–19). One night shortly after his arrival, Somers walks into the bush and feels the presence of "something big and aware and hidden" that fills him with "terror," the terror that any civilized and "conscious" European—whether or not he favors the Lawrencian primeval, "blood-consciousness," or the unconscious—must feel in the presence of so pure and enormous an embodiment of the unconscious:

> But the horrid thing in the bush! He schemed as to what it would be. It must be the spirit of the place. Something fully evoked tonight, perhaps provoked, by that unnatural West-Australian moon. Provoked by the moon, the roused spirit of the bush. He felt it was watching, and waiting. Following with certainty, just behind his back. It might have reached a long black arm and gripped him. But no, it wanted to wait. It was not tired of watching its victim. An alien people—a victim. It was biding its time with a terrible ageless watchfulness, waiting for a far-off end, watching the myriad intruding white men. (19)

The presence is supernatural, but certainly not necessarily benign. Our problem is reconciling Somers's reaction to it as a "horrid thing" with his desire near the end of the novel, as strong as "wanting a woman" (382), for a place in the bush. The solution to the problem is that the bush is both an ambiguous and a developing symbol. Somers's thinking about it changes or develops as his acquaintances with Kangaroo and Jack and Willie Struthers progressively persuade him of the inadequacy of a love worked entirely through the spirit or "consciousness"; that is, through the "white man's" will.

As Somers regards the bush on the train journey to Coo-ee the first time, it has similarly equivocal qualities, but now they shade into the positive. In the bush spreading toward the Blue Mountains lurks the "strange, as it were, *invisible* beauty of Australia" that is "just beyond the range of our white vision." The landscape is "unimpressive, like a face with little or no features, a dark face . . . so aboriginal." It is indeed like the aboriginal, whose face is "ugly" and "distorted" yet aglow with "wonderful dark eyes that have such incomprehensible shine in them, across gulfs of unbridged centuries" (87). The bush then is what we have lost—it holds our ancient selves, our primitive, unconscious beings before we became "outward," before we became "white." The bush and the Cornish moors run parallel in Somers's thought. We have already seen how their "shagginess" was like "the fur of some beast." "The Nightmare" describes how, as Somers "sat there on the sheaves in the under-dark . . . , he felt he was over the border, in another world" (263). He is across that Australian "gulf of unbridged centuries." Somers realizes that "he no longer wanted to struggle along, a thought adventurer," but to "drift into a sort of blood-darkness, to take up in his veins again the savage vibrations . . . of the pre-Christian human sacrifice." His desire is to cut loose from "his own white world, his own white conscious day" (264). He finally, of course, cannot: he is a "thought adventurer" and he will not give up his "real, civilized consciousness." He realizes nonetheless how this civilized consciousness (with that governing word "real") must be conditioned by the "half-conscious" world (264), must contain it as the shell contains the seed.

In the last chapter, "Adieu Australia," Lawrence describes the bush at its loveliest and at its most terrifying. The description is the apt culmination of the novel's *symbolic* action. Somers and Harriet pay their last visit to the bush. Beauty and lushness alternate with barrenness:

> The thorny wattle with its fuzzy pale balls tangles on the banks. Then beautiful heath-plants with small bells, like white heather, stand in tall, straight tufts, and above them the gold sprays of the intensely gold bush mimosa, with here and there, on long thin stalks like hairs almost, beautiful blue flowers, with gold grains, three-petalled, like reed-flowers, and blue, blue with a touch of Australian darkness. Then comes a hollow, desolate bare place with empty greyness and a few dead, charred gum-trees, where there has been a bush-fire. At the side of this bare place great flowers, twelve feet high, like sticky dark lilies in bulb-buds at the top of the shaft, dark, blood-red. Then over another stream, and scattered bush once more, and the last queer, gold red bushes of the bottle-bush tree, like soft-bristly golden bottle-brushes standing stiffly up, and the queer black-boys on one black leg with a tuft of dark-green spears, sending up the high stick of a seed-stalk, much taller than a man (389).

About it all were "the utter loneliness, the manlessness, the untouched blue sky overhead . . . , the age-unbroken silence of the Australian bush" (390). They come to a "thick green of strange trees narrowing into water." It is a terrifying place, where "the water fell in a great roar down a solid rock, and broke and rushed into a round, dark pool . . . low down in a gruesome dark cup in the bush." Here the stream disappears, shut in by rock and bush: "The river just dived into the ground." The description is superbly horrible, intensified by the suggestion of the presence of snakes: "It was a dark, frightening place, famous for snakes." Somers has a "horror of them in the air, rising from the tangled undergrowth" (390). But at last the Somerses emerge, Harriet with an armful of brilliantly blooming bush plants. Back at Coo-ee Harriet says that this experience has been "the loveliest thing" she has known: "They were both silent. The flowers there in the room were like angel-presences, something out of heaven. The bush! The wonderful Australia" (391).

The descriptions incorporate through symbol the chief thematic developments of the novel. Somers has been the "snake"; he has been of the devil's party. His dark, ithyphallic God, speaking from the inward caverns of his unconscious, is nonetheless the core of our "real civilized consciousness." If the "gruesome cup" in the bush (symbolically, if not geographically, the heart of the heart of the bush) with its tangled undergrowth and "horror" of snakes is a frightening region, it is also a place of the loveliest beauty, of "angel-presences, something out of heaven." Lawrence's renderings of the bush with its attendant imagery make it a brilliantly forceful symbol for the way that the unconscious self (as Lawrence perceives it) informs and enriches our conscious lives and for the way that our negation of this self makes "bits" of us. In the chapter "Bits," Somers reflects on the "man by himself. The listener." The problem is that "most men can't listen any more. The fissure is closed up. There is no soundless voice" (311). But the fissure *is* open and the "soundless voice" does speak to the individual who dares approach it, horrible (and beautiful) though it be, as Somers does in this last, deftly encapsuling and climactic scene. *Kangaroo* is indeed a wilderness adventure, and if its "blood being" is not recognizable among the known or seen creatures of the animal kingdom, it is nonetheless the "presence" that haunts and informs, from its place within, those actions that make up the outer part of Lawrence's down-under novel. The art of *Kangaroo* lies in Lawrence's attentive orchestration of metaphor and symbol from the beginning. The subtext grows from what seems at first merely throwaway details. But these are much more than the rubbish "bits" that litter the surface of the Australian landscape and by symbolic extension form the surface of Western consciousness: they are the essential bits that create the unifying subtexture or subsurface of the whole—the inside that gives meaning to the outside.

Chapter 5

St. Mawr and Its Metaphors
The Making of Meaning and Coherence

From the standpoint of the critical responses it has generated, *St. Mawr* is the most interesting of Lawrence's novellas. For one thing, it has had its grand extravagant admirer in F. R. Leavis, who on the basis of its "creative and technical originality" compared it favorably to *The Waste Land*.[1] His views sparked a debate in *Essays in Criticism* in the mid–1950s. Since then the tale has had a number of considerate readings, and as with nearly all those works of Lawrence after *Women in Love*, there has been no clear consensus about its standing as a work of art. Graham Hough, in his ambivalent assessment that *St. Mawr* is in some respects "among Lawrence's most brilliant performances," yet not "an authentic piece of work," suffering as it does from a "falsity in the motive and the conception that fatally affects the whole," probably speaks for a majority of critics, who also admire the execution of several of its parts but cannot approve, say, either the coherence of its symbols or the logic of its structure. Martin Jarrett-Kerr (Father William Tiverton) describes *St. Mawr* as "bi-valvular," the England first part and New Mexico second part having little relation to one another. Eliseo Vivas, though he believes that when Lawrence sticks to presenting St. Mawr he achieves "a vivid and powerful revelation," finds it nonetheless "incomprehensible" that anyone could consider the book excellent. For Vivas, *St. Mawr* is "very close to the worst" of Lawrence's works. He speaks of the story's "essential inchoateness," charging that Lawrence failed to find an "adequate symbol" for dramatizing the conclusion's "metaphysical abstractions."[2]

Discussions of the meaning of *St. Mawr* have also proved interesting. The first two-thirds or so of the story presents no problem. We seem to be confidently balanced on the predictable Lawrence keel of attacking the English (and modern civilization in general) while contending for the forgotten or beleaguered primitive forces or dark gods. But when the action is transported to the American Southwest, we may well experience a sense of dislocation. For not only does the setting shift, but so do the tone, style,

1. Leavis, *D. H. Lawrence: Novelist*, 279
2. Hough, *The Dark Sun: A Study of D. H. Lawrence*, 180; Jarrett-Kerr, *D. H. Lawrence and Human Existence*, 75; Vivas, *D. H. Lawrence: The Failure and the Triumph of Art*, 151–52, 161–62.

and seemingly even the mode of the novel. Feeling as Dr. Johnson might have, we may well be troubled to have bought into a comedy and instead discovered ourselves bound for some destination other than the one we had anticipated.

To be sure, not all of Lawrence's critics are bothered greatly by the "bivalvular" aspect of the structure nor by the apparent shift from one set of meanings to another. Several critics have provided valuable backgrounds or approaches by which we can better come to grips with this shift and these meanings. Keith Sagar in *D. H. Lawrence: Life into Art* gives a remarkably full accounting of Lawrence's movements and reading together with those letters and the accounts of others that generate for us a context for the work. Moreover, his discussion of Lawrence's knowledge of Indian folklore and myths in general surrounding the horse goes a long way toward helping us see some of the unities in the story. James C. Cowan's discussion of the duality of the story helps us see how the symbolic dimensions of the New Mexico setting in the conclusion are a broadening and deepening of the symbolic dimensions of St. Mawr. His being dropped from the action, Cowan argues, is not a problem but an important "index to Lou's maturation" in that, "rather than becoming fixated at one stage of development, she is able to relinquish even the source of her inspiration to the fulfillment of his own [St. Mawr's] instinctual being and to continue her own creative growth in the life newly opened to her." The best pure study of Lawrence's narrative strategies in *St. Mawr* is that of Alan Wilde. Wilde says that the narrative appears, on first reading, "to be chaos itself," without plot and with little story. The problem then, he contends, involves the work's "formal integrity," and its solution "requires the exploration of the techniques Lawrence employed to shape his work." This accomplished, it "becomes easy not only to understand why the horse is dropped so casually from all notice, but also to see what vision of life the book as a whole means to communicate."[3]

Though not always in complete agreement,[4] these attempts to elucidate *St. Mawr* and to authenticate it as a coherent work of art are, it seems to me, almost totally successful. Yet *St. Mawr* is a work that, because of its mixture of styles, its distension of narrative, and the extreme Lawrencian density of its meanings, is always going to provoke intense disagreement and ambivalent feelings. R. E. Pritchard, for instance, writing after both

3. James C. Cowan, *D. H. Lawrence's American Journey: A Study in Literature and Myth*, 96; Wilde, "The Illusion of *St. Mawr:* Technique and Vision in D. H. Lawrence's Novel," 164.

4. For instance, Cowan rejects Wilde's claim that "the one absolutely false note" in the novel results from Lou's statement about the need of the "wild spirit" for her (Cowan, *American Journey*, 96; Wilde, "Illusion of *St. Mawr,*" 169).

Wilde and Cowan, calls it "a work of great power but of uncertain meaning and doubtful success. Perhaps its most apparent weakness lies in the uneasy relationship between symbolic action and realistic surface: certainly both plot and characters are improbable." Pritchard, as a psychological critic, in a way brings a more objective opinion to the specialized concern of *St. Mawr's* artistic success than do these others since he is interested more nearly in explaining Lawrence than in measuring the formal or "literary" success of the novel.[5] My point is that Lawrence's fiction is various enough, offering so many interesting avenues of understanding and appreciation, that although we will usually agree as to whether a particular work is of major or minor importance, we will invariably find ourselves disagreeing about it in relation to these other considerations.

This presence of seemingly opposed and irreconcilable elements itself causes readers to pronounce certain works "ambiguous" and even "incoherent." We find this true from work to work also. How totally unlike, say, are *Kangaroo* and *St. Mawr* in formal narrative technique. And how unlike and therefore confusing in the attempt to understand Lawrence's ethic are the central developments in *The Plumed Serpent* and *Lady Chatterley's Lover*. The particular work, then, becomes a synecdoche or microcosm of Lawrence's fiction as a whole during his last decade, and the *apparent* incoherence of a *Kangaroo* or a *St. Mawr* seems to epitomize or underline a more general and therefore damning incoherence within the *corpus*. Is this body sick, after all, as many have argued, its organs laboring in confusion against one another? I think not. To be sure, one does find incoherence: *The Plumed Serpent*. But one diseased organ does not a corpse make. At bottom is an amazing integrity, or health, and as I have advised, our best approach to understanding it is to attempt to understand Lawrence's imagery, his strategic management of metaphor. Just as the incoherent imagery of *The Plumed Serpent* reveals an incoherent novel, so the coherence of imagery within *St. Mawr* reveals (and helps to make) a greater coherence. Lawrence's surfaces may indeed put the unwary off: the real meanings are *inside*—in more ways, of course, than one. The subtext, as we have seen with *Kangaroo*, holds the key to the text.

Lawrence did not choose his metaphors. That is to say, given the direction that his ideas took about society and the relation of the individual to it, these being founded upon his personal experiences, the imagery came about quite naturally as the perfectly organic expression of his feelings. We

---

5. Pritchard, *D. H. Lawrence: Body of Darkness*, 157. On the other hand, Pritchard might be considered mainly a layman in this matter of aesthetic appreciation. Certainly he has not read the work as carefully as he might. He confuses, for instance, the wretched Dean Vyner, of all characters, with the artist Cartwright, who of course is modelled on Frederick Carter.

can look back to *Aaron's Rod* as perhaps the pivotal novel in the process whereby this imagery originates, for a curious thing happens there. Where Lawrence usually creates one character, in *Aaron's Rod* he creates two who are D. H. Lawrence: Aaron Sisson and Rawden Lilly.

The novel has Aaron go through the experiences that lead to his becoming Lilly, who has already gone through his own variation of them. On first observation, it might seem that Lilly, the writer, is the more public, more revealed individual, and Aaron, who is already in flight from his family, is the more covert, more recessive one. But not so. Lilly has learned the tricks of camouflage, of keeping his head down; Aaron has yet to learn these tricks and still presents himself to the cross hairs of modern civilization even as he retreats from it.[6] As I have argued, *Aaron's Rod*, coming almost precisely in mid-career both chronologically and in terms of works produced, marks the major transition in Lawrence's life as a writer. Prior to *Aaron's Rod*, no matter what their propensities toward a private life and withdrawal, Lawrence's protagonists are individuals who live *in* the world, have positions or responsibilities that bring them into frequent contact with others, or are seen in familial contexts: Paul Morel (clerk), Ursula Brangwen (teacher), and Rupert Birkin (school inspector). In the later works, the Lawrence-figures tend to be already confirmed isolates, not individuals merely moving in that direction: Count Dionys in "The Ladybird," Richard Lovat Somers in *Kangaroo*, Morgan Lewis in *St. Mawr*, Cipriano in *The Plumed Serpent*, Oliver Mellors in *Lady Chatterley's Lover*, and the risen Christ in *The Escaped Cock*. To be sure, one or two are more "public" than others—Cipriano in his role as military officer, Somers as a socially engaged writer. Notably, however, each of these is defined less by the public context than by his seeing the frustrations or futility of a life within that context. *St. Mawr* is one of Lawrence's most forceful representations of this fact. Composed in two drafts (the first destroyed by fire) in the summer of 1924, *St. Mawr* records the depth of Lawrence's disillusionment with society. It stands, beyond its own considerable merits, as a significant postscript or epilogue to *Kangaroo*. Its development, as we shall see, especially as figured in its imagery, makes it a sort of *Kangaroo* in miniature.

Like the other novels of Lawrence's last decade, *St. Mawr* seeks to sort out the "real" world, as we might call it (since Lawrence does), from the unreal. In Texas, Lou Carrington wonders, "What was real? What under heaven was real?" (132). She can find "no roots of reality at all. No consciousness below the surface. . . . Visually, it was wildly vital. But there

---

6. An early fictional instance of an event that provoked this extreme wariness, or distrust, occurs in *Women in Love* when Halliday mockingly recites to the clique in the Pompadour Cafe a letter he has received from Birkin. In reality it was *Amores* that Halliday-Heseltine mocked spitefully in the Cafe Royal.

was nothing behind it" (131). Certain words in this passage are obviously significant: *reality, consciousness, vital.* Equally significant, though submerged in their functions as metaphor or preposition, are *roots, below, behind.* For Lou sees that only what happens within, in the "deeper consciousness" (131), is reality; the rest is merely "visually" real, or "surface," therefore "nothing." That Lawrence's prepositions, with the more usual nouns, verbs, adverbs, and adjectives, should become themselves metaphors indicates something interesting not only about the way that language in general works but also about the way that Lawrence's language is organically inseparable from the story's deepest truths.

St. Mawr makes Lou aware of the life she is not living. Like her, he "was not quite happy" (28). Lou knows she has to buy him, but not for the usual reasons that a person wants to buy a horse. Rather, it is "as if that mysterious fire of the horse's body had split some rock in her." She can only cry from her recognition of the void that is her life. "The wild brilliant, alert head of St. Mawr seemed to look at her out of another world" (30). He is at once "god" and "splendid demon" looming "out of the everlasting dark" with a "non-human question." She feels that "she must worship him" (31). Lawrence puts himself in a somewhat precarious position with these statements, the one in fact for which he is most often attacked. But he makes it quite clear that he is aware of the implications of this position. The problem, of course, is that he must assert the primacy of the "animal life" without asserting that the animal is primary. Thus, Lou later describes the way "the animal in [men] has gone perverse, or cringing. . . . I don't know one single man who is a proud living animal" (61). But Lou does not wish to be misunderstood: "I don't want to be an animal." She does not "admire the cave man, and that sort of thing," for she does not ignore, or diminish, thought. It is only that men "have left off really thinking. But then men always do leave off really thinking, when the last bit of wild animal dies in them" (61).[7]

For Lawrence, thinking occurs in the whole individual. The head and the body are extensions of one another, not discrete or separable. They are

7. We can nearly always substantiate our inferences about Lawrence's fiction from his nonfiction written at about the same time. Thus, in "Books" (1923; unpublished during Lawrence's life), Lawrence verifies the inference (confirmed by internal evidence from the story) that it is not blood against intellect but blood *with* intellect that he is advocating in *St. Mawr*: "Man finds that his head and his spirit have led him wrong. We are at present terribly off the track, following our spirit, which says how nice it would be if everything was perfect, and listening to our head, which says we might have everything perfect if we would only eliminate the tiresome reality of our obstinate blood-being. We are sadly off the track, and we're in a bad temper, like a man who has lost his way. And we say: I'm not going to bother. Fate must work it out. Fate doesn't work things out. Man is a thought-adventurer, and only his adventuring in thought rediscovers a way" (*Phoenix*, 732). Lou is thus finding her way, not by leaving intellect behind in England, but by grounding it in her "blood-being" in New Mexico.

separable only in one like Rico, who epitomizes "modern youth" with its show of surfaces; clothes (the visible as opposed to the unseen) and music (the audible as opposed to the sweeter inaudible) are the features that define modern youth's values. Of Rico, Lawrence writes: "If his head had been cut off, like John the Baptist's, it would have been a thing complete in itself, would not have missed the body in the least" (34). Rico's opposite number is Lewis, the groom, who, though he may appear to be without "intelligence," actually blends the animal, or bodily, self with a higher consciousness. But Lawrence first wants to establish Lewis within the under-world of the "animal" domain. Thus he stares "from between his bush of hair and beard, watched like an animal from the underbrush." Rico, whose face is "always perfectly prepared for social purposes" and is naturally not to be imagined "unshaven, or bearded, or even mustached," is properly apprehensive of Lewis. He "was still sufficiently colonial to be uneasily aware of the underbrush" (34), just as he is of St. Mawr. It is a battle of two worlds. Lewis tells Lou to meet St. Mawr "half-way": "But half way across from our human world to that terrific equine twilight was not a small step. It was a step, she knew, that Rico would never take. . . . But she was prepared to sacrifice Rico" (35). We have something like this, then: Rico, the purely conscious self, is "uneasily aware" of the unconscious self, repelled, it would probably be safe to say, by it. Lou, on the other hand, is attracted, even fascinated, by the subterranean element she sees in St. Mawr and is prepared to sacrifice Rico, the sterile ego, in pursuit of it. This is not to say that she is going to relinquish the conscious or rational self. It is to say that she recognizes intellect by itself to be a dead end, as Rico has become for her.

In the preceding passages, Lawrence is establishing his duality or dichotomy of the "two worlds," the human and the animal. But stated in this bare way, the dichotomy is so simplistic as to make almost no sense. It is through description, through metaphor primarily, that the dichotomy breaks open into several other clarifying divisions or oppositions: surface-subterranean, outer-inner, over-under, higher-lower, visible-invisible, light-dark, heard-unheard. (Though some of these pairs may sound nearly identical, they are distinctive.) The second term of each pair is the positive, expressing what is to be desired. Each of these is parallel or synchronous with the others, and together they provide the amplifications and qualifications that give artistic dimension to the human-animal dichotomy. The fact that these dichotomies very often work beneath the surface or literal level of language and meaning only enriches our pleasure in the story. But when we are distracted by the seemingly too-obvious satirical language and fail to see how the images reinforce or qualify one another, we are apt to misread or read superficially by not treating Lawrence seriously enough.

In just the few passages examined thus far, the reader sees how the metaphors accomplish the task. The "mysterious fire" splitting the rock in Lou is an appropriately sexual image to signify her awakening. The rock is "in" Lou, just as the fire comes from within the horse's "body." Whatever her questions and doubts, Lou from this point on lives from the bedrock of herself (as her husband's life is all *on* the surfaces). The horse seems to look at her from "out of" another world, that is, from *within* another world. He looks at her "out of the everlasting dark." His look then is "demonish" and "non-human." The man who takes his nourishment from these sources would be a "pure animal man . . . burning like a flame straight from *underneath*" (my italics) both "unseen" and "silent." Lewis, being such a man, watches these people "like an *animal* from the *underbrush*" (my italics). We see how these images resonate against one another, pick one another up, so that they wear not only their own meanings but take on the others' as well. Lewis's hair, as previously noted, is described as a "bush," identifying him further with the deeper, hidden world of nature suggested in the description of his eyes, which are those "of a wildcat peering intent from *under* the darkness of some *bush* where it lies *unseen*" (33; my italics). A few pages later, Mrs. Witt is reflecting upon Lewis's statement that he would never shave his beard off because it was "a part of him":

> "Isn't that extraordinary, Louise?" she said. "Don't you like the way he says *Mam*? It sounds so impossible to me. Could any woman think of herself as Mam? Never!—Since Queen Victoria. But, do you know it hadn't occurred to me that a man's beard was really part of him. It always seemed to me that men wore their beards, like they wear their neckties, for show. I shall always remember Lewis for saying his beard was part of him. Isn't it curious, the way he rides? He seems to sink himself in the horse. When I speak to him, I'm not sure whether I'm speaking to a man or to a horse." (38)

The contrast between the necktie, a purely external ornament, and the beard, which grows internally from roots, points up the difference between the modern world, as represented by Rico, and the ancient, primitive world embodied in Lewis. The one is always outer, artificial; the other inner, real. Lewis, significantly, "sinks himself in the horse," in the real (because inner) world, in the "source," which is the unconscious. For that reason, Lou tells her mother, he has a "real mind" that "knows things without thinking them," not a merely "clever," superficial mind, like Dean Vyner's.

The discussion of Pan that takes place at Dean Vyner's, though it elaborates the dichotomy through several of the metaphors (stated and implied), achieves its effect principally through the visual metaphor. The artist Cartwright, whose face resembles the "Great Goat" Pan's, says that the "Great God" Pan is "the God that is hidden in everything. In those days you saw the thing, you never saw the God in it: I mean in the tree or the fountain or the animal." You would die if you saw Pan, except at night: "In the daytime you see the thing. But if your third eye is open, which sees only the things that can't be seen, you may see Pan within the thing, hidden: you may see with your third eye, which is darkness" (65). This seems murky at best until one realizes that by seeing with the "third eye" Lawrence means seeing as Maurice Pervin of "The Blind Man" sees—intuitionally. The third eye is "darkness" after all; it is the animal, the instinctive, the unconscious, the inner, buried self. It sees darkness, those things that are buried or whose source is "hidden," coming from within or beneath. Thus, the three images Cartwright mentions: the tree has roots in and the fountain emerges from the earth, from *under* the ground. Similarly, the animal is "lower," instinctual, and usually lives hidden or submerged in nature, often in darkness.

The symbolic details of the expedition to the Devil's Chair and its dramatic aftermath enlarge on the meanings here and show what happens when the third eye does not open. "It was one of those places where the spirit of aboriginal England still lingers, the old savage England" (73). It is here, appropriately enough, that Mrs. Witt, whose third eye *is* coming open, fixes the "fair young man" with a "demonish straight look." He has responded to Lou's "We don't exist" (in contradistinction to those who once "worshipped devils among these stones") with "I jolly well know *I* do" (74). Mrs. Witt says, "I should like *so* much to know what makes you so certain that you exist?" (75). Shortly, as if to prove to us that he does not, he begins to whistle a "new dance tune" (Lawrence despised, of course, contemporary popular music) that Rico finds "awfully attractive." This noisy insult seems to be the climax of all the insults to the unheard and unseen presences, the devils in the stones. It is as if they at last exact their revenge through St. Mawr, who rears and falls back on Rico (he will not let go) and then kicks the fair young man in the face (that is, in the mask that he wears), disfiguring him. It is the "under" rising against the over, the inner striking the outer. Plainly, the unconscious or animal self (St. Mawr) is rising against the superficial ego of the modern age (Rico and the fair young man). The conscious self that disclaims the unconscious self cannot survive intact. Nor can the unconscious self restrain its inevitable potential for violence, even evil. Lou's encounter along the roadside with a snake crushed by stones reinforces the symbolism. The dead snake is the id crushed by the Ricos of the world. Lawrence probably relished giving Rico and the fair young man their just deserts; the scene, nonetheless, is done descriptively, not didactically or in summary. The meaning comes through

in the subtext. Lou, St. Mawr's advocate and admirer, has no excuses for
him. The event has been purely evil on all sides, as Lou's "vision" makes
plain:

> It was something horrifying, something you could not escape from.
> It had come to her as in a vision, when she saw the pale gold belly of the
> stallion upturned, the hoofs working wildly, the wicked curved hams of
> the horse, and then the evil straining of that arched, fish-like neck, with
> the dilated eyes of the head. Thrown backwards, and working its hoofs in
> the air. Reversed, and purely evil.
>   She saw the same in people. They were thrown backwards, and
> writhing with evil. And the rider, crushed, was still reining them down.
> (78–79)

Cowan believes that the central action of *St. Mawr* pivots upon the duality
of mind and body, of the "lower sensual plane" and the "upper spiritual
plane of consciousness."[8] I would say that *St. Mawr* has two main actions
or lines of development. Certainly, one is the duality that Cowan is concerned with and that I have been concerned with so far on the level of its
attendant imagery. But from this point on, the novel goes in two directions.
With Mrs. Witt and Lewis, it investigates further the mind-body dichotomy.
With Lou and Phoenix and the New Mexico ranch, it investigates the lower
sensual plane, seeking to find and define those distinctions that will give
credibility and authority to the Lawrencian ethic.

Before moving to this second development, however, we might observe the way that the attraction Mrs. Witt comes to have for Lewis is
described through this prepositional imagery. Before Mrs. Witt leaves with
Lewis for Oxfordshire, she and Lou make plans for saving St. Mawr from
Rico and Flora Manby, who wish to castrate him. As Lou remarks, Flora
"goes straight to the root of the matter." Mrs. Witt adds, "And eradicates the
root" (97); that is, takes *out* what is *in*. Revolting against her previous life,
Mrs. Witt now begins to fear she will die the wrong kind of death: "To pass
out as she had passed in, without mystery or the rustling of darkness! That
was her last, final, ashy dread." She longs, rather, "to die . . . *positively*: to
be folded then at last into throbbing wings of mystery, like a hawk that
goes to sleep. Not like a thing made into a parcel and put into the last
rubbish-heap" (102). "Ashy" and "rubbish heap" are just right; they are
external, visible remains. And she is not placed *inside* a parcel, but made
into one, so that again the externality of the thing is its chief feature.
Lawrence renders her desires in imagery precisely opposite: she wants to
be "folded into" the wings of darkness "like a hawk that goes to sleep."

8. Cowan, *American Journey*, 86.

Thus, she enters what itself goes *in*—she into the throbbing darkness of the wings of the hawk, which itself enters sleep, a compounding of effect that also blends or merges categories (animals and color) of imagery.

Just as Lou seeks the real, so does Mrs. Witt at last. She seeks it in Morgan Lewis: "And yet, what made him perhaps the only real entity to her, his seeming to inhabit another world than hers. A world dark and still, where language never ruffled the growing leaves, and seared their edges like a bad wind" (104). This passage complements the earlier scene in which St. Mawr reacts violently to the fair young man's whistling. All of Lawrence's mature work features in greater or lesser degree a tension between the worlds of light and darkness, the visible and invisible. But in *St. Mawr* he takes us one sense further, one "world" further. Lawrence's method is nearly always accretion. He might have stopped with a "world dark and still." But the reader of Lawrence expects accretion, elaboration, a further manipulation of detail. Three paragraphs later, the reader gets it: "The visible world, and the invisible. She had lived so long, and so completely, in the visible, audible world. She would not easily admit that other, inaudible" (104). Often this sort of reinforcing by Lawrence is thought to be clumsy and unnecessary, and sometimes it is. But here the elaboration justifies itself. It takes us further and further in, just as Mrs. Witt desires to be taken further into the world of Morgan Lewis. The prepositional prefixes help sink us more deeply within the world of darkness and silence, as Mrs. Witt desires to be sunk in the world of Morgan Lewis, as he himself does "sink" into St. Mawr. The metaphors that Mrs. Witt evokes for him after he has repulsed her serve to locate him further in the animal or, more broadly, the natural world. He is "unapproachable as a cactus," a "little cock-sparrow" (112). Lawrence writes that "he did not care about persons, people, even events. In his own odd way, he was an aristocrat, unaccessible in his aristocracy. But it was the aristocracy of the invisible powers, the greater influences, nothing to do with human society" (121).

As stated at the outset of this chapter, the "Lawrence figures" after *Women in Love* increasingly seek camouflage from the "greater" world of society. Lawrence's language complements this retreat inward and downward, *away* from society. Thus Lou seeks "retreat to the desert," an image that becomes a brilliantly accurate metaphor and symbol as Lawrence develops it in the last part of the story. Lou and Lewis, as the similarity of their names hints, are part of the same phenomenon or essence, though we see that for Lou it still exists in the stage of desire or potential and for Lewis in the stage of realization. I do not believe it to be accidental either that the name of each has a phonetic kinship with *Lawrence*.[9] He was also

9. Keith Brown relates Lawrence's meeting with Jaime de Angulo, a scholar of Ameri-

"in retreat," a phrase that is not pejorative since the retreat is also a quest: inward toward the dark gods, often referred to now as "demons" (the devil being conventionally represented, of course, as living in the bowels of the earth). Thus, when Lawrence writes that St. Mawr lifts his head "like a bunch of flames" (64), we understand he does so because he is "a dark god looking . . . out of the everlasting dark." He is "some splendid demon, and she must worship him" (31). "Demons upon demons [are] in the chaos of his horrid eyes." Why, then, "did he seem like some living background, into which she wanted to retreat?" (41). Critics like Vivas have lashed Lawrence for his "incoherence" in this novel, for the disjunction between the New Mexican conclusion and the England beginning and middle. But the reader sees plainly here how Lawrence cements connections through his language, his imagery. The horse *is* "horrid," yet Lou's impulse. The ranch is an extension of St. Mawr that offers opportunities for a more thorough and complex investigation. There, too, the "demon" imagery continues. The ranch has its pine tree, a "demonish guardian, from the far-off crude ages of the world" (144). Its flowers bloom red, "as if the earth's fire-centre had blown out some red sparks" (150).[10] The action and the imagery conduce to a terrific unity. It was a shrewd and courageous decision on Lawrence's part not to bring Lewis (with St. Mawr) to Las Chivas. For Lewis, singular as he is as a characterization, is not quite real. As a (only seemingly unlikely) *raisonneur*, he is perfect; as a character, he lacks dimension. And his presence might have softened the harsh answers that the "spirit" of this place gives back to Lou's questions. Instead he brings Phoenix, who embodies many of the same brutal—and brute—qualities of the place.

Phoenix, after all, is merely the other side of Rico, not the *inside* of him. If Rico is surface intelligence without the deeper, animal consciousness, Phoenix is animal sensuality unredeemed by any other consciousness. Rico is sexuality mentalized; Phoenix is the "sexual rat" (137), nature wholly and merely sensual. The entire continuum of Rico-Phoenix is vicious; that is, Lou would not be satisfied with a man at the midpoint of this spectrum and would still throw in her faith with the Vestal Virgins. Sensuality is merely another kind of surface: "She understood now the meaning of the Vestal Virgins, the Virgins of the holy fire in the old temples. They were symbolic of herself, of woman weary of the embrace of incom-

---

can Indian mythology, who probably told Lawrence about Loo-Wit, the protagonist in the most famous of the Indian volcano myths. Lou's name, if Brown is right, surely comes from the Indian myth. But I think also, on the subconscious level at least, it is self-reflexive as well.

10. Sagar illuminatingly identifies the devil with the pagan fertility God Cernunnos, "the Celtic horned god of the beasts, who can also be identified with Pan" (*D. H. Lawrence: Life into Art*, 259–60).

petent men, weary, weary, weary of all that, turning to the unseen gods, the unseen spirits, the hidden fire, and devoting herself to that, and that alone. Receiving thence her pacification and her fulfilment" (138–39). Whatever form the incompetence takes, Rico's or Phoenix's, Lou's recourse as she sees it is to turn to the "unseen gods" lest she become corrupted also. The metaphor with which Lawrence describes this development in Lou works in terms, once again, of inner and outer. Of her past relationships and of her marriage to Rico, Lawrence writes: "And what of it all? Nothing. It was almost nothing. It was as if only the outside of herself, her top layers, were human. . . . Within these outer layers of herself lay the successive inner sanctuaries of herself. And they were inviolable" (139). Lou's retreat, then, takes place within two geographies. She retreats into the inner geography of the soul, to the "old temples" there, the "unseen spirits," the "hidden fire," the "successive inner sanctuaries of herself." At the same time, she has retreated from the outer, social layers of civilization, as represented by England, into the inner, original, "presexual" world, as represented by New Mexico, "the world of the gods unsullied and unconcerned [that] lived its own life" (146). Lawrence clearly intends each retreat to reflect the other. But Las Chivas is also clearly a further dimension of Lou's retreat into the successive inner sanctuaries of herself and as such is a deepening of the novel's central action, taking on meanings not altogether anticipated by the first three-quarters of the novel.

At first, however, it seems as if the American West is intended purely as objective correlative for the vestal changes in Lou:

> She felt a great peace inside herself as she made this realisation. And a thankfulness. Because, after all, it seemed to her that the hidden fire was alive and burning in this sky, over the desert, in the mountains. She felt a certain latent holiness in the very atmosphere, a young, spring-fire of latent holiness, such as she had never felt in Europe, or in the East. "For me," she said, as she looked away at the mountains in shadow and the pale-warm desert beneath, with wings of shadow upon it: "For me, this place is sacred. It is blessed." (139–40)

She soon realizes, in the next paragraph in fact, that considerably more is involved:

> But as she watched Phoenix: as she remembered the motor-cars and tourists, and the rather dreary Mexicans of Santa Fe, and the lurking, invidious Indians, with something of a rat-like secretiveness and defeatedness in their bearing, she realised that the latent fire of the vast landscape struggled under a great weight of dirt-like inertia. She had to mind the dirt, most carefully and vividly avoid it and keep it away from her, here in this place that at last seemed sacred to her. (140)

We now see the reason for Phoenix: he personifies the "rat-like" qualities, the "dirt" she must keep herself free from if she is to maintain her own inner sacredness, which seems mirrored by the sacredness of the landscape. More than mirrored: connected. As she tells her mother at the end, "And I am here, right deep in America, where there's a wild spirit wants me, a wild spirit more than men. And it doesn't want to save me either. It needs me. It craves for me. And to it, my sex is deep and sacred, deeper than I am, with a deep nature aware deep down of my sex. It saves me from cheapness, mother" (155). Wilde finds the notion of the spirit's wanting her a false note.[11] But why should it be? Although Lawrence has said that the "great circling landscape lived its own life, sumptuous and uncaring. Man did not exist for it" (146), we are to understand that Lou's development is toward precisely this same condition: "I'll tell you—and you mustn't get cross if it sounds silly. As far as people go, my heart is quite broken. As far as people go, I don't want any more. . . . I want to be alone, mother" (153). She wishes no more contact until "my taking a man shall have a meaning and a mystery that penetrates my very soul" (155). Lou's statement that her "sex is deep and sacred," then, expresses a recognition based upon her "deep nature"—with emphasis on *both* words—the deepness and sacredness of her sex. While the other English characters (Lewis, of course, excepted) have de-natured themselves, Lou has been *naturing* her being.

To help us understand this wild spirit, this myth, of place and its duality, especially its harsh, "sordid," "repulsive" aspect, we might recall the visit by Richard Lovat Somers and Harriet to the "fern world" at the end of *Kangaroo*. Here they are given a glimpse, as it were, into the savage bowels of creation. What they perceive is both lovely (the marvelous Australian flowers) and "frightening" (390):

> By the stream the mimosa was all gold, great gold bushes full of spring fire rising over your head, and the scent of the Australian spring, and the most ethereal of all golden bloom, the plumy, many-balled wattle, and the utter loneliness, the manlessness, the untouched blue sky overhead, the gaunt, lightless gum-trees rearing a little way off, and sound of strange birds, vivid ones of strange, brilliant birds that flit round. Save for that, and for some weird frog-like sound, indescribable, the age-unbroken silence of the Australian bush. (389–90)

As they go deeper, they come to the place where "the river just dived into the ground": "It was a dark, frightening place, famous for snakes. Richard hoped the snakes were still sleeping. But there was a horror of them in the

11. Wilde, "Illusion of *St. Mawr*," 169.

air, rising from the tangled undergrowth, from under the fallen trees, the gum-trees that crashed down into the great ferns, eaten out by white ants" (390). Lawrence does not develop the horror, but now in *St. Mawr*, he describes this horror in some considerable detail, dramatizing it through the New England woman's encounter with the pack rats and black ants, the hell that is only suggested by the "fang-mouthed" flowers (148). To be sure, there is loveliness, and Lawrence's descriptions of the landscape are among his finest. But finally the savagery and the sordidness overcome the woman, who succumbs to the "century-deep deposits of layer upon layer of refuse: even of tin cans" (151). Moreover, we remember in *Kangaroo* that the chief outward manifestations of this inner sordidness were the litter of tin cans everywhere. So the New England woman leaves, defeated, and the "old" England woman arrives. She will win because she can meet, even admire, the savagery on its own terms. The sordidness she knows about, as she is aware of the men "so grovelling and ratty" (153); having had it in her own system, she has purged it. So it is the "spirit" that needs her.

As noted in the previous chapter, *Kangaroo* suggests that Lawrence had been influenced by the texture and seemingly digressive manner of development in *Moby-Dick*, which he had written about not long before in *Studies in Classic American Literature*. Poe, another author that he treats there, may also have been an influence, though we do not know if he had read *Narrative of A. Gordon Pym*. It hardly matters if he had not. The interesting and important thing is the way the two endings replicate an archetypal pattern. The course of Pym's journey south into the Antarctic takes him progressively deeper into a starkly primitive setting that on the symbolic level resembles a journey into the unconscious. As Pym's boat approaches the mystic center, a vapor arises, becoming quickly dense. The winds are fierce, but "soundless." And then this from the last entry in Pym's journal:

> The darkness had materially increased, relieved only by the glare of the water thrown back from the white curtain before us. Many gigantic and pallidly white birds flew continuously now from beyond the veil, and their scream was the eternal *Tekeli-li!* as they retreated from our vision. Hereupon Nu-Nu stirred in the bottom of the boat; but, upon touching him, we found his spirit departed. And now we rushed into the embraces of the cataract, where a chasm threw itself open to receive us. But there arose in our pathway a shrouded human figure, very far larger in its proportions than any dweller among men. And the hue of the skin of the figure was of the perfect whiteness of the snow.[12]

12. Poe, *The Narrative of A. Gordon Pym*, in *Collected Writings of Edgar Allan Poe*, 1:205–6.

In descending into the elemental center of nature, Pym seems to have encountered the presiding god, or demon, or spirit of the place. It is a remarkable description, one of the strangest and most fascinating in literature. Lou's journey, similarly, takes her progressively deeper into nature, into the elemental, and though she encounters no abominable snowmen or snow gods, she does meet with the same presiding genius encountered by the New England woman. When the violent thunderstorm had sent its "rivers of fluid fire" to the earth, the New England woman was made to know "secretly and with cynical certainty, *that there was no merciful God in the heavens*." Each time she sees the white scar left on the pine tree by the lightning her unconscious self says: "*There is no Almighty loving God. The God there is shaggy as the pine-trees, and horrible as the lightning*" (147). The figure approximates Pym's. It may be terrible and shaggy, like nature itself, but it is marvelous, too, "*more awful and more splendid. I like it better*"; that is, better than the god of love. The reward is mixed. The ranch offers "life, intense bristling life, full of energy, but also with an undertone of savage sordidness" (147–48). It is this sordidness that defeats the New England woman.

Lawrence says a few pages later that "all savagery is half-sordid" and that "man is only himself when he is fighting on and on, to overcome this sordidness" (151). This statement is essential Lawrence. And it contains a certain paradox of imagery that should help those who have misunderstood Lawrence to see that the life he is after all in pursuit of is a higher, not a lower, one. The paradox is that one's salvation, the higher life, lies in going *in* or *down* and that the lower life, the merely savage and therefore sordid one, is the result of the failure to attempt this inward descent or journey. Thus, "every civilization, when it loses its *inward* vision and its cleaner energy, falls into a new sort of sordidness" (151; my italics). It is no accident that the Devil's Chair in Wales is higher than the Angel's Chair. When Mrs. Witt asks Louis why they are not going to the Angel's Chair, he answers, "There's nothing to see there. The other's higher, and bigger." Mrs. Witt replies, "Is that so!—They give the Devil the higher seat in this country, do they? I think they're right" (73).

Lou's retreat is to the south and west, to the desert mountains. Pym's psychic journey takes him due south, to the southern extremity of the world, where he meets the spirit—god or demon, or both—of this world. Ahab's mad quest takes him south also, where "the deepest blood being of the white race," as Moby Dick is described in *Studies in Classic American Literature* (160), kills him because he tries to kill it. Lou's journey, though south, is to the mountains—we descend to the higher life. The "shaggy" and "horrible" spirit there is, of course, a demon-god. Nietzsche's Zarathustra also retreated to the mountains, where he lived with his serpent and eagle before going down again to show that the way to the overman is by "going under."[13] Thus, we have the terrible fire that seems to come out of St. Mawr and the one that rains out of the sky above the New Mexico ranch. As St. Mawr in England acts out his nature, so Lou in New Mexico acts out the saving knowledge she has acquired. In Lawrence's essay "On Human Destiny" (1923), we find a passage that brings together a number of the things I have been discussing. Here Lawrence describes how in "the howling wilderness of slaughter and debacle, tiny monasteries of monks, too obscure and poor to plunder, kept the eternal light of man's undying effort at consciousness alive" (*Phoenix II*, 627). Lou, in the same effort, has formed a monastery (or convent) of one. In another passage from "On Human Destiny," the imagery and ideas trace those of the development in *St. Mawr*:

> As a thinking being, man is destined to seek God and to form some conception of Life. And since the invisible God *cannot* be conceived, and since Life is always more than any idea, behold, from the human conception of God and of Life, a great deal of necessity is left out. And this God whom we have left out and this Life that we have shut out from our living, must in the end turn against us and rend us. It is our destiny. Nothing will alter it. When the Unknown God whom we ignore turns savagely to rend us, from the darkness of oblivion, and when the Life that we exclude from our living turns to poison and madness in our veins, then there is only one thing left to do. We have to struggle down to the heart of things, where the everlasting flame is, and kindle ourselves another beam of light. In short, we have to make another bitter adventure in pulsating thought, far, far to the one central pole of energy. We have to germinate inside us, between our undaunted mind and our reckless, genuine passions, a new germ. The germ of a new idea. A new germ of God-knowledge, or Life-knowledge. (*Phoenix II*, 627–28)

Among all the correspondences with St. Mawr—the rending of Rico by "the God we have left out" (by St. Mawr), the "everlasting flame" that comes from "the heart of things" (from St. Mawr and the New Mexico sky)—perhaps the most striking is the reference to "the one central pole of energy." Lou's revelation comes upon reaching, in New Mexico, her "central pole." There is also a correspondence with the revelation to Pym of God at the moment he reaches the South Pole.

None of Lawrence's novels incorporates myth more effectively than *St. Mawr*. *The Plumed Serpent* tries harder but achieves, for all its length, much less. It is this effective assimilation of myth that dissolves the charge that *St. Mawr* is "bi-valvular." To be sure, however, it is bipolar. The poles

---

13. Nietzsche, *Thus Spoke Zarathustra*, in *The Portable Nietzsche*, 122.

are not "animal" and "human" but the "real" and the "unreal." Lou's journey, her "thought-adventure," is a retreat from the one and a quest for the
other. The New Mexico ranch and mountains, with their shaggy god, constitute the symbol for this pole, as St. Mawr and the Devil's Chair are
symbols for the stages in the journey, each containing an aspect of the
polar destination. These are the chief parts of the remarkable symbolic
dimensions of the novel. But there is a second dimension that undergirds
the symbolic, that creates further unity: the metaphorical dimension. In
the first part of the novel, when Lawrence is being his most "satirical," and
in the last part, when he is being his most "metaphysically abstract," the
imagery is constant. It is the imagery of Lawrence's dichotomies, of the
inner and outer, the lower and higher, of interiors and surfaces—in short,
of the real and unreal. The reader, to approach meaning, descends along
the ladder of Lawrence's metaphors, down their nouns and verbs, adjectives and adverbs, even, as we have seen, the lowly prepositions, to the
subtext where he then may rise, as Lou does from her descent to the wild
indwelling spirit, to understanding. Hence we share Lou's thought-adventure and Lawrence's "pulsating thought."

Chapter 6

The Imagery of *The Plumed Serpent*
The Going Under of Organicism

The Plumed Serpent has this distinction: it is D. H. Lawrence's most ambitious failure. William York Tindall, who hardly admired Lawrence anyway, is very nearly alone in believing the work to be his best. Other readers, including Katherine Anne Porter, praise the writing in the novel or in portions of it, and perhaps a very few, most notably L. D. Clark, who is hardly reticent about the book's problems, would prefer to think of it as a qualified success rather than as an interesting failure.[1] The great majority, however, take this latter view—or worse. Eliseo Vivas, though he allows that the book has several "virtues," thinks its central situations "silly." David Cavitch considers them "offensive." Julian Moynahan calls its rituals "bathetic." Graham Hough believes that the novel simply "goes to pieces." Even F. R. Leavis finds the book hard to stomach; he speaks of it as the only one of Lawrence's novels "difficult to read through." James C. Cowan speaks for most of these critics when he criticizes *The Plumed Serpent* for its failure of unity.[2] The central defect of the book, according to the overwhelming majority of the critics, is that its parts simply do not hang together organically. Thus, Leavis says that it is "willed and mechanical," and Vivas that it is not an "organic work of art."[3] Of these critics, only Cowan and Clark concern themselves with the imagery. Neither, however, discusses the imagery in relation to the novel's problems. Like the others, they trace its failure largely to implausibilities in plot, character, and meaning, as well as to Lawrence's lack of success in integrating these elements. Though so much is true, I believe that the best clue to why *The Plumed*

1. Tindall, *D. H. Lawrence & Susan His Cow*, 13; Porter, "Quetzalcoatl," 262–67; Clark, *The Dark Night of the Body: D. H. Lawrence's "The Plumed Serpent."* In her review, Porter praises Lawrence's "immense and prodigal feeling for the background," for making "every minute detail" appear as though "seen with the eyes of a poet" (264). Her objections are the usual ones, however: the hymns of Quetzalcoatl are mainly "hollow phrases" (266) and his central characters "mouthpieces" (267). Reading *Sons and Lovers* again, she says, will make us "realize the catastrophe that has overtaken Lawrence".
2. Vivas, *D. H. Lawrence: The Failure and the Triumph of Art*, 70; Cavitch, *D. H. Lawrence and the New World*, 109; Moynahan, *The Deed of Life: The Novels and Tales of D. H. Lawrence*, 109; Hough, *The Dark Sun: A Study of D. H. Lawrence*, 129; Leavis, *D. H. Lawrence: Novelist*, 69; Cowan: *D. H. Lawrence's American Journey: A Study in Literature and Myth*, 120.
3. Leavis, *D. H. Lawrence: Novelist*, 69; Vivas, *Failure and Triumph*, 72.

Serpent goes wrong lies in Lawrence's handling of its imagery; when the imagery begins to go wrong, so does the novel.

In considering Lawrence's description, Clark makes a useful if awkward distinction between what he calls "ordinary description" and "organic description": "Organic description, as I am using the term, includes the body and spirit of the principal character involved: both in his individual and in his allegorical capacity, and the spirit of religious awareness embodied in the landscape—in 'nature' if you will." According to Clark, chapter 5, "The Lake," contains several instances of organic description in which "the dominant force of Lawrence's genius expresses itself."[4] Any image deserving to be called organic must present, of course, at least the appearance of having participated in a lived experience. It is true that the talented author can make us believe that a scene in which a character participates must be one that the author has similarly experienced—even if this is not the case. Thus, the incidents involving the snake near the end of the novel and those with the urchin and waterfowl earlier give the impression of having happened. The images grow out of the action; they do not appear merely to have been superimposed upon it. The problem is that these scenes of "organic description," as Clark speaks of them, are more nearly incidental than central; the principal imagery, nearly all of it symbolic, is, though brilliant in conception, of the "ordinary" sort. Here we see that Lawrence's failure to make the characterizations of Don Ramón and Cipriano and their actions plausible has a corollary failure in imagery. Because we finally cannot believe in the imagery, which is made to carry much of the meaning of the novel, we cannot believe in the characters and their deeds, and the novel caves in on itself. Nonetheless, Lawrence is working with an exceedingly ambitious imagery. For a long while, our fascination with its symbolic configurations and with its complex and largely successful interconnections is sufficient to distract us from the growing problems of character and action. The first part of this chapter will examine the extent to which this central imagery is successful and will consider one very likely source for the imagery. The second part will investigate what goes wrong. I will be exploring, in short, why the first half or so of the novel seems to work, then why the second half does not.

I

There are, of course, two central actions in *The Plumed Serpent*: the reestablishment of primitive religion and culture in Mexico and the real-

4. Clark, *Dark Night*, 56.

ization of what we might call a Lawrencian womanhood for Kate. Lawrence works hard to bring these two actions within one frame; given the effort that he must have put into it, we should not find it difficult to see why he thought it, at one stage of its composition, the novel that "lies nearer my heart than any other work of mine" (*Collected Letters*, 2:844). The two main actions, integrated through Kate's relationship with and ultimate marriage to Cipriano together with her assumption of the role of the green goddess Malintzi, parallel a third action, that of the developing symbolic imagery of the novel. One of the problems is Lawrence's failure to synchronize properly the imagery and the two principal actions of the plot. But purely in terms of how much he gave himself to do and how intricate the apparatus necessarily became, we cannot but admire the magnitude of the task, if not the final product itself.

As with just about all of Lawrence's later works, *The Plumed Serpent* has its source and being in myth. The best examinations of the mythic dimensions are those of Clark and Cowan.[5] Both directly confront the way in which the central symbol, the circle, either synthesizes or embodies Lawrence's principal thematic concern of integration, or "creative being."[6] If one statement from the novel succeeds in connecting the two actions, it is Kate's (later echoed by Constance Chatterley): "Ye must be born again" (61). Kate, of course, is born again, as is Quetzalcoatl. Kate's effort for herself (as well as Don Ramón's for the Mexican people) is nothing less than an attempt to come full circle to the lost condition of integrated being. In addition to emblematizing wholeness, then, the circle structurally embraces the central actions of the novel.

The most important images involved in Lawrence's circling symbolism are either themselves not circles or have symbolic meanings that extend beyond the circular. To this first category belong the snake, the eagle, the "Tree of Life." To the second belong the sun, the morning star, the eye. Related also to several of these is associative, subordinate imagery that reinforces and amplifies the meanings of the main symbols. So rich (if finally incoherent) are the parts making up the whole of *The Plumed Serpent* that, for all the critical attention paid to the novel, much remains to be said, especially about the imagery. To consider, as I am doing here, Lawrence's strategy regarding several of the images is merely to scratch the overall surface. The question is why, if this novel is a failure, we should

5. John B. Vickery, "*The Plumed Serpent* and the Renewing God," and Jascha Kessler, "Descent into Darkness: The Myth of *The Plumed Serpent*," are also valuable, Vickery's study in demonstrating the influence of Frazer upon the symbol and structure of the novel and Kessler's in demonstrating the presence in *The Plumed Serpent* of the monomythic pattern that Campbell delineated in *The Hero With a Thousand Faces*.
6. Cowan, *American Journey*, 103.

wish to irritate that surface further. The answer, of course, is that we often have as much to learn about an author and his technique from his failures, especially when they are ambitious ones, as from his successes. Certainly, this novel tells us much about Lawrence's method in his later novels. Clark's analysis of the way the symbolic conclusion of the novel plays against the beginning at the bull ring and the way the symbol of the lake throughout establishes a texture and a reference point reveals that Lawrence has certainly devised here, as in the previous works, impressive strategies involving the coordination of details.[7] Consequently, his efforts along these lines deserve our consideration. In fact, the evidence of the two drafts of *The Plumed Serpent* indicates that it is one of Lawrence's most deliberated novels.

The symbols of the eagle and the snake, which in the Quetzalcoatl emblem form the eyelike circle, recall for us, as Julian Moynahan has remarked, the unicorn-lion opposition of "The Crown" and the iris symbol of *The Rainbow*.[8] The one is our higher, the other our lower consciousness. Although Don Ramón Carrasco is the "representative" of Quetzalcoatl, whose symbols are *both* eagle and snake, he is also the eagle (with his European, "white" consciousness) to Cipriano's snake (with his Indian, "dark" consciousness). One of Cowan's criticisms is that, though Lawrence suggests balance as the ideal, he generally subordinates the one to the other: "This duo-mythic pattern, through the metaphorical function of contrasting characters, is employed in differentiating between white consciousness and dark consciousness as opposite modes of being. The effect of the contrast, however, rather than to reconcile the two, is to elevate the latter at the expense of the former."[9] Cowan's contrasts are Ramón-Cipriano versus Owen Rhys-Bud Villiers, Teresa versus Carlota, Ramón versus the Bishop. But when we view the opposition in terms of the eagle (or bird) and the snake, this criticism, though probably still valid for a good portion of the book, is not quite so easy to make. *The Plumed Serpent* contains much genuine criticism of the dark, instinctual self. Again and again we read of the "serpent-like," "reptilian" oppression of the spirit of Mexico. Kate thinks with revulsion of the "reptilian," "half-created women": "Something lurking, where the womanly centre should have been; lurking snake-like. Fear! The fear of not being able to find full creation, . . . insolent against a higher creation, the same thing that is in the striking of a snake" (77). Cipriano, despite his education, has a "barbarian consciousness," which is like an "intolerable weight" upon Kate. Clearly, he needs Kate, as

7. Clark, *Dark Night*, 72–73, 140–43.
8. Moynahan, *The Deed of Life: The Novels and Tales of D. H. Lawrence*, 108–9.
9. Cowan, *American Journey*, 100.

he needs Don Ramón to complete his being. For, unlike Ramón, he is all snakelike darkness.

In general, however, the novel vigorously posits blood-instinct and not mind-spirit as the way through. The tenor of nearly all of Don Ramón's screeds is that we must throw off the Christian spiritual ethic by submerging ourselves in the instinctual life. Implicit in this descent is an ultimate reconciliation, but the novel's pronouncements, whether we view them in Don Ramón's or in Cipriano's statements or in Kate's attempt to synthesize these with her own more cautionary attitudes, are heavily on the side of "blood knowledge." This much is evident in Lawrence's selection of the two creatures that together take on the shape of the novel's central symbol. Lawrence, of course, is more or less stuck with the snake if he is going to give the myth of Quetzalcoatl primary status in the novel. His selection of the eagle as complement to the snake is considerably more arbitrary. The fact that he chose the fiercest, most rapacious of the avians (when he might have chosen, say, the dove) makes the novel's predispositions quite clear—and this is a problem with the novel: whereas in *Kangaroo* a tension always pulses up through the prose, here the action and the outcomes seem, indeed, *predisposed*. Clark, who has much to say about both images, assumes that Lawrence's selection of the eagle, since it figures in the Mexican flag, was practically automatic. I would suggest as amplification to Clark, not in contradiction of him, that Lawrence was also thinking of Nietzsche, who figures importantly in Lawrence's attitudes during this period.[10] To be precise, the snake and the eagle, which are the emblems of Quetzalcoatl, are also the emblems (and companions) of Nietzsche's Zarathustra.

Before pursuing this association further, I would like to look at the way in which Lawrence conflates eagle and snake and eye into one artistically complete symbol. In "The Plaza," before the participants form the inner and outer dance rings (symbolizing among other things the dark sun within the outer sun), Lawrence describes the leaflet upon which Kate and we encounter the first of many poems of Quetzalcoatl:

> At the top of the leaflet was a rough print of an eagle within the ring of a serpent that had its tail in its mouth: a curious deviation from the Mexican emblem, which is an eagle standing on a nopal, a cactus with great flat leaves, and holding in its beak and claws a writhing snake.
>
> This eagle stood slim upon the serpent, within the circle of the snake, that had black markings round its back, like short black rays pointing inwards. At a little distance, the emblem suggested an eye. (118)

10. In this regard, see my article "D. H. Lawrence and Friedrich Nietzsche." *Philological Quarterly* 53 (1974): 110–20.

Then follows the poem:

> In the place of the west
> In peace, beyond the lashing of the sun's bright tail,
> In the stillness where waters are born
> Slept I, Quetzalcoatl.
>
> In the cave which is called Dark Eye,
> Behind the sun, looking through him as a window
> Is the place. There the waters rise,
> There the winds are born.
>
> On the waters of the after-life
> I rose again to see a star falling, and feel a breath on my face.
> The breath said: Go! And lo!
> I am coming. (119)

The rest of the poem concerns the withdrawal of Jesus to make way for the reemergence of Quetzalcoatl. Of concern to us here, however, is the way that Lawrence forges the four images into one comprehensive symbol of the higher (here deeper) vision celebrated by the Romantics. Addressing the assemblage, Ramón tells of Quetzalcoatl's emergence from the lake and what he said to the thirsty men who came to hear him. Having assured them that he brings moisture for their dry mouths, he says: "When the snake of your body lifts its head, beware! It is I, Quetzalcoatl, rearing up . . . and reaching . . . to the sun of darkness beyond, where is your home at last." He tells them, "Without me you are nothing. Just as I, without the sun that is back of the sun, am nothing" (123). Lawrence provides a number of reinforcing scenes and incidents. Earlier Kate, feeling the old "so-called reality" starting to give way, experiences "a soft world of potency . . . in its place. . . . Behind the fierce sun the dark eyes of a deeper sun were watching, and between the bluish ribs of the mountains a powerful heart was secretly beating, the heart of the earth" (109). Here Lawrence is taking the image beyond itself, as he will do elsewhere, to suggest the organic connection possible when we see with more than what Blake calls "single Vision and Newton's sleep." Later, at his house, Ramón, backgrounded by the sun, appears to Kate dressed as Quetzalcoatl. On his hat is a round crest "like an eye, or a sun" (170). The emblem devised by Ramón's blacksmith is of a bird within the sun, whose circle, of course, replicates the snake. The sail of Ramón's *canoe* "had the great sign of Quetzalcoatl, the circling blue snake and blue eagle upon a yellow field, at the centre, like a great eye" (284). Kate is never of one mind about the movement, though her doubts do diminish and her acceptance grows—enough certainly for her to marry Cipriano and to take on the brideship of Malintzi. But early in the novel she felt "like a bird round whose body [the Mexican] snake has coiled itself" (72). As Ramón had told her in a metaphor we shall examine later, "It may be you need to be drawn down, down, till you send roots into the deep places again. Then you can send up the sap and the leaves back to the sky, later" (80).

This passage leads nicely into Nietzsche and into the remarkable analogies between *The Plumed Serpent* and *Thus Spoke Zarathustra*. The title character of Nietzsche's eccentric work is a figure who in special regards is rather like Kate herself and also like Ramón-Quetzalcoatl. Like Kate (and like other Lawrencian heroes), he has an almost obsessive fear of and loathing for humanity. He urges the higher types to "flee into your solitude! You have lived too close to the small and miserable. Flee their invisible revenge!" Humanity is so many "poisonous flies," and it is "far from the market place that the inventors of new values have always dwelt."[11] Yet like Kate and Ramón Carrasco, he needs companions:

> For a long time Zarathustra slept, and not only dawn passed over his face but the morning too. At last, however, his eyes opened: amazed, Zarathustra looked into the woods and the silence; amazed, he looked into himself. Then he rose quickly, like a seafarer who suddenly sees land, and jubilated, for he saw a new truth. And thus he spoke to his heart:
> "An insight has come to me: companions I need, living ones—not dead companions and corpses whom I carry with myself wherever I want to. Living companions I need, who follow me because they want to follow themselves—wherever I want." (135)

The similarities here to the Quetzalcoatl situation in *The Plumed Serpent* are intriguing to say the least. Like Quetzalcoatl, Zarathustra returns to the world after a considerable absence. In his instance, to be sure, it is not an age but a decade; nonetheless, like Quetzalcoatl, he arises after a lengthy sleep to urge a renewal upon the world. Again like Quetzalcoatl, he will restore by pulling down the old values: "The man who breaks their tables of values, the breaker, the lawbreaker; yet he is the creator" (135). Quetzalcoatl, of course, is a deity of pre-Christian origins whose vitality as a god lies deep within the primitive roots of Mexican-Indian culture; Zarathustra, similarly, is rooted in the ancient pre-Christian past. Under his more common name, he is the Persian prophet whose teachings became the foundation for Zoroastrianism. In seeking an ethic or religion in opposition to Christianity, both authors significantly locate its source in primitive civi-

---

11. Nietzsche, *Thus Spoke Zarathustra*, in *The Portable Nietzsche*, 164–65. Further citations of this work are indicated parenthetically in the text.

lizations. The prophet (Zarathustra) and the god (Quetzalcoatl) predictably preach a human, earth-based religion. Here is Zarathustra:

> Behold, I teach you the overman. The overman is the meaning of the earth. Let your will say: the overman *shall be* the meaning of the earth! I beseech you, my brothers, *remain faithful to the earth*, and do not believe those who speak to you of otherworldly hopes! Poison-mixers are they, whether they know it or not. Despisers of life are they, decaying and poisoned themselves, of whom the earth is weary: so let them go.
>
> Once the sin against God was the greatest sin; but God died, and these sinners died with him. To sin against the earth is now the most dreadful thing, and to esteem the entrails of the unknowable higher than the meaning of the earth. (125)

To acquire what is needed, he, like the sun, must "go under": "I must descend to the depths, as you do in the evening when you go behind the sea and still bring light to the underworld, you overrich star. Like you I must *go under*—go down. As is said by man, to whom I want to descend" (122).

The "overman," of course, is Kaufmann's translation of *Ubermensh*, a more accurate rendering than "superman" in that it preserves the over-under tenor of Nietzsche's ethic. As Quetzalcoatl, Don Ramón's efforts are to create his own cadre of overmen. He tells Cipriano, "I would like to be one of the Initiates of the Earth. One of the Initiators. Every country its own Savior. . . . And the First Men of every people forming a Natural Aristocracy of the World. One must have aristocrats, that we know. But natural ones, not artificial" (248). Nietzsche's attack upon Christianity also centered on its artificiality. It was, in his view, an antinatural religion. Precisely the same is true for Lawrence. Thus, Zarathustra's "God is dead" has its analogue in the retirement from Mexico of the moribund Christ. The reborn deity, like his followers, must as Zarathustra says, "go under." As Don Ramón told Kate, "It may be you need to be drawn down, down, down, till you send roots into the deep places again" (80). There is even a hint of Nietzsche's notion of eternal recurrence in the alternation of Quetzalcoatl and Jesus as Mexico's deities, for centuries earlier a worn-out Quetzalcoatl had withdrawn as quietly and resignedly as Jesus does now. "*Quetzalcoatl said*: It is very good. I am old. I could not do so much. I must go now. Farewell, people of Mexico. Farewell, strange brother called Jesus. Farewell, woman called Mary. It is time for me to go" (222). The rhythms of life dictate the rise and fall of religions. The implication is that Quetzalcoatl's present emergent triumph is subject still to cyclical decline.

All of this has been preamble to an examination of the prologue of *Thus Spoke Zarathustra*, a line or two of which I have just quoted above.

The prologue contains the basic shape of the Quetzalcoatl development in *The Plumed Serpent*, and it contains all of the core images of that novel:

> When Zarathustra was thirty years old he left his home and the lake of his home and went into the mountains. Here he enjoyed his spirit and his solitude, and for ten years he did not tire of it. But at last a change came over his heart, and one morning he rose with the dawn, stepped before the sun, and spoke to it thus:
> "You great star, what would your happiness be had you not those for whom you shine?
> "For ten years you have climbed to my cave: you would have tired of your light and of the journey had it not been for me and my eagle and my serpent.
> "But we waited for you every morning, took your overflow from you, and blessed you for it.
> "Behold I am weary of my wisdom, like a bee that has gathered too much honey; I need hands outstretched to receive it.
> "I would give away and distribute until the wise among men find joy once again in their folly, and the poor in their riches.
> "For that I must descend to the depths, as you do in the evening when you go behind the sea and still bring light to the underworld, you overrich star.
> "Like you I must *go under*—go down, as is said by man, to whom I want to descend.
> "So bless me then, you quiet eye that can look even upon an all-too-great happiness without envy!
> "Bless the cup that wants to overflow, that the water may flow from it golden and carry everywhere the reflection of your delight.
> "Behold, this cup wants to become empty again, and Zarathustra wants to become man again."
> Thus Zarathustra began to go under. (121–22)

Like Ramón's Quetzalcoatl, Zarathustra must take up a human existence if his influence is to be vital. Quite remarkable is the appearance here of the images that in *The Plumed Serpent* become the central symbols: the eagle and the snake, the sun-star, the rendering of the sun as an eye, even the lake and the image of restorative water. To be sure, Nietzsche does not develop these images as Lawrence does. Nonetheless, they signal vitality. Eagle and snake, as in Lawrence, effect the reconciliation between transcendence (spirit) and descendence (instinct). In Lawrence, of course, the morning star further establishes the notion of a balance between the two ways. The sun here has no dark counterpart, but Nietzsche insinuates much the same idea when he speaks of its nightly descent "to the depth" of the sea "underworld." If the sun, like an "eye," has by day a "vision," so by night, through its "going-under," it takes on the property of a further, deeper vision. Nietzsche, like Lawrence, is insistent that if man is to achieve an organic relation to the universe, he must see with more than the purely rational eye. Finally, Zarathustra speaks of the lake he left and the waters with which he once again would like to refill his cup for the regeneration of others. Quetzalcoatl returns to earth from a lake, and water throughout the novel signals regeneration. Certainly it is no surprise to discover that water symbolizes life or renewal (it would be surprising if it did not). It is surprising, however, to find these conjunctions of images in such a short space in a work otherwise so similar in meaning to another. If Lawrence was not consciously or unconsciously influenced by *Zarathustra*, then we have, I think, a remarkable coincidence that would seem to validate the theories of Frazer, Jung, and others who have worked with mythic and archetypal figures—that is, the belief that an elemental presence in our subconscious selves informs our conscious way of seeing the world. It may be that artists do not so much choose among what there is in what they work with as that they have no choice in what they "choose." The important consideration then becomes not so much what they write about as how they write about it. This question, as it concerns these images and others in *The Plumed Serpent*, will be the focus of the second part of this chapter.

II

The central thematic opposition in *The Plumed Serpent*, as in some sense it is in all of Lawrence's fiction, is the opposition between organic connection and mechanical fragmentation. We have observed Kate as she realizes that she must break with the "sterility of nothingness which was the world, and into which her life was drifting," that she must free herself from her mechanical connections with people like Villiers, who were "widdershins, unwinding the sensations of disintegration and anti-life" (113). Her new life is to be bound up in Don Ramón, who speaks for and leads the cause of vital religion, and in Don Cipriano, whose dark, Pan-like nature is the fleshly embodiment of Ramón's speeches. The language of these speeches, as we have seen, puts a high premium upon symbol. But in the speeches and conversations and also in the language of the novel there is a satellite imagery that never becomes symbol. The function of this imagery is to reinforce the theme of organicism. The central images are bird (flight, flock), tree or plant (forest, leaf, sap), heart (blood), and water (lake, ocean, rain). We get an idea of how Lawrence intends this imagery from this passage from a speech by Ramón:

> "Put yesterday's body from off you, and have a new body. Even as your God who is coming, Quetzalcoatl, is coming with a new body, like a star, from the shadows of death.

"Yes, even as you sit upon the earth this moment, with the round of your body touching the round of the earth, say: Earth! Earth! you are alive as the globes of my body are alive. Breathe the kiss of the inner earth upon me, even as I sit upon you.

"And so, it is said. The earth is stirring beneath you, the sky is rushing its wings above. Go home to your houses, in front of the waters that will fall and cut you off forever from your yesterdays.

"Go home, and hope to be Men of the Morning Star, Women of the Star of Dawn.

"You are not yet men and women—"

He rose up and waved to the people to be gone. (200)

That is, they will never be "men and women" until they consent to be born again. But it is the imagery as well as the meaning which concerns us here. Just about all of the imagery of this passage conveys a vitalistic picture of the surrounding world. But the principal image, it seems to me, is not that of the earth in vegetable stir or the sky "rushing" like a bird or even the purifying rains. Rather it is the image of the earth and body as globes. These images serve the novel's central symbol, the circle. Lawrence has Ramón speak of the "round of your body touching the round of the earth," and then: "Earth! Earth! you are alive as the globes of my body are alive." The globe is a wonderful image because it connects two things between which there must be an organic relation. Moreover, it does so through an image that unobtrusively suggests fruit, which, of course, in one form or another is the climax and goal of the entire system of organic life. Our perception of what Lawrence has done here is not so much rational as it is imaginative or intuitive. If Ramón's speeches are usually prose, this one is poetry. Finally, the passage combines in some way or other each of the central images I have spoken of above, taking on the character of a synecdoche for the vast organic relationship toward which its speaker is striving.

Lawrence's chief image of organicism is hardly original: the Tree of Life. In the first ceremony that takes place in the plaza, Kate thinks of what is happening to her as "a sort of fate" she cannot resist. She thinks, "Like fate, like doom. Faith is the Tree of Life itself, and the apples are upon us," the apples of the eye, chin, heart, breast, belly "with its deep core," loins, knees, even "the little, side-by-side apples of the toes" (126–27). She perceives that change and evolution do not matter: "We are the Tree with the fruit forever upon it. And we are the faith forever. Verbum Sat" (127). Only Kate in this novel is capable of thinking these words; Ramón, except by fluke or authorial lapse, would be incapable of them. There is a certain whimsy, if not humor exactly, about them, which relieves them of the sententiousness they might otherwise have. The wordplay ("apples of the eye," "apple of the belly, with its deep core") and the inclusion of chin, knees, and "little, side-by-side apples of the toes" give the paragraph a kind of charm. Here are the great and small—heart and loins, but also chin and knees and toes. These globes are all a part of the fine organic "round" which is Man Living.

This paragraph is followed by one which combines the myriad satellite images in a manner similar to the "globe" passage:

> The one singer had finished, and only the drum kept on, touching the sensitive membrane of the night subtly and knowingly. Then a voice in the circle rose again on the song, and like birds flying from a tree, one after the other the individual voices arose, till there was a strong, intense, curiously weighty soaring and sweeping of male voices, like a dark flock of birds flying and dipping in unison. And all the dark birds seemed to have launched out of the heart, in the inner forest of the masculine chest. (127)

The extended avian metaphor commences with a description of the birds (voices) taking off separately, alone ("one after the other") and concludes with a description of them as one (a "flock"). The last sentence of the paragraph, in which the many voices come as if from a singular chest, presages the union of men that is to come with the renewal of the myth of Quetzalcoatl in the hearts of the people. But the people will have one heart then, just as the disparate images—bird, heart, trees ("inner forest")—are fused here in one trope. This is an alert piece of writing, the images quietly but efficiently encapsuling the larger meaning of the book.

Lawrence's vegetable imagery strategically parallels the dualistic animal imagery of eagle and snake. Each image is intended to signify the necessity of a balance between the higher and lower, or the spiritual and physical (sexual, instinctive), faculties of man. Ramón-Quetzalcoatl says, "My stem is in the air, my roots are in all the dark" (226). Kate, when she is dancing in the revolving circles, begins "to learn softly to loosen her weight, to loosen the uplift of all her life, and let it pour slowly, darkly, with an ebbing gush, rhythmical in soft, rhythmic gushes from her feet into the dark body of the earth" (132). The "ebbing gush" suggests both water and blood. These images then fuse with the vegetative in the next sentence: "Erect, strong like a staff of life, yet to loosen all the sap of her strength and let it flow down into the roots of the earth" (132). This imagery replicates the meaning of the eagle-snake imagery. But in the merging of imagery from different elements, Lawrence accomplishes something further, as we have observed: he reinforces our sense of the organicism of the cosmos. It *is* a vitalistic earth that Lawrence wants to convey. When he has Ramón-Quetzalcoatl say of the "snake of the world" that "only his living keeps the soil sweet, that grows your maize" and that "the trees have root in him, as the hair of my face has root in my lips" (196), he is once again epitomizing the relation among all living things (vegetable, animal, human) through the merging relations of these images themselves.

So far so good. The problem is that it does not go very much further. To be sure, there are a number of nice touches we can admire, as Clark, Cowan, and others have pointed out. The snake and the foal episodes in the last two chapters are both brilliantly concrete dramatizations of Kate's wishes first to submit and then not to submit. The difficulty is that these scenes and others finally do not carry the weight of the meaning but are subordinate or incidental to it. It is ironic, I suppose, that a novel that works so hard for the cause of organicism finally fails, according to the charges of Vivas and others, because its own parts do not themselves achieve an artistic organic relation.

I remarked earlier that the novel's failure is attributable to Lawrence's failure to sustain a consistent imagery. The second half of *The Plumed Serpent* has going for it several instances of fine descriptive writing, which we expect from Lawrence, together with the tension (what there is of it) achieved through Kate's indecisiveness. Nonetheless, the latter portion is, by common consent, a bore. The most glaring defects are, first, the extremes to which Ramón and Cipriano take their ideas and, second, the finally stale repetitiveness of Ramón's oratory and ideas. The extravagances that occur in the second half of the novel—the ritual executions and the "marriage" of Kate-Malintzi to Cipriano-Huitzilopochtli being the chief but not the only instances of these—impair if not destroy our confidence not only in the characters and the narrative but also in the novel's larger meaning and purpose. Moreover, the novel's lame credibility by this point is not bolstered by the later poems and speeches. For, if we have not heard them before, we *think* we have heard them before. And the new development in that plot, the marriage between Malintzi and Huitzilopochtli, is really an anticlimax or, worse, a serious derangement in the coherence of the novel's central tension and attendant imagery.

What happens, I believe, is that Lawrence fails to synchronize the imagery and the action. Thus, while symbol (eagle and snake) and metaphor (tree-stem and roots) assert a balance à la "The Crown" between mind-spirit and blood-instincts, the action is already moving along a logic insistent upon the superiority of the dark forces of the primitive self. Though "Quetzalcoatl" claims that he is "lord of two ways," the "master of up and down," whereas Christ had been lord but "of the one way" (228), more and more it appears that Ramón-Quetzalcoatl is the lord of the *other* way: down. No synthesis of Carlota's Europeanized-Christian "way" with Ramón's primitive-pagan way is allowed. Lawrence has madness kill her off. Teresa, who replaces Carlota, is a Ramón look-alike. Ramón, who had seemed the eagle complement to Cipriano's snake, becomes Cipriano's look-alike. He may wear, as Quetzalcoatl, the blue of the sky as opposed to the red and black and earth colors that Cipriano wears as Huitzilopochtli, but it is the moral colors of Huitzilopochtli's serpent code that Ramón actually wears. In the strange ceremony in which Cipriano becomes "the living Huitzilo-pochtli" late in the novel, the priest or conductor who initiates him is Ramón. Over and over he asks Cipriano, "It is dark?" (367–68). Finally, of course, fully initiated, Cipriano sees that it is "all dark," "perfect." All that remains is for Ramón and Cipriano to conduct Kate, as the "green Mal-intzi," to her marriage-in-darkness with Cipriano-Huitzilopochtli. To be sure, green is her color, and grass is the product of both blue air and yellow sun, on the one hand, and the dark "under-earth" (375) on the other. But her allegiance must be utterly to the latter. She is, in fact, Persephone to Cipriano's Pluto, as in "Bavarian Gentians." Though Lawrence connects Cipriano with Pan and not Dis, he is, nonetheless, her demon lover, and as his wife, she must have as her realm the darkness "of the ancient Pan world, where the soul of woman was dumb, to be forever unspoken" (312). Hardly a synthesis, then—mind, soul, light extinguished, gone "dumb" in the gravitational pull of Cipriano's "Demon-power" (312).

Had Lawrence not established the logic of another imagery, another symbology, our fault-finding here would be of little weight. As it is, we are struck by a glaring inconsistency between design and execution. More-over, Lawrence's orchestration of his main symbolism climaxes prema-turely. In the first half of the book, the skill with which he introduces and then develops the imagery is fascinating. We are, indeed, witnessing a master hand at it, that of one of the twentieth century's finer poets. (Cer-tainly the real poetry in the novel is in the prose, not in the "poems.") The problem is that he brings the development of this imagery to its crisis before the main actions in the plot even take place. This point is what I mean when I say that the failure of the novel can be blamed upon a failure in the management of the imagery, a failure to coordinate imagery and action. Had Lawrence been successful in pacing his imagery and in em-bodying the action in the images (and vice-versa), the result might have been the artistic whole promised by the early chapters. By contrast, in Aaron's Rod, imperfect as that novel is, Lawrence orchestrates his imagery with the action. Aaron does not throw his rod into the river halfway through the narrative. When he does, it comes with appropriate symbolic signifi-cance, as does Lilly's remark near the end that the broken rod (also Aaron by extension), having organic properties (it is said to "blossom"), can re-generate. In Lady Chatterley's Lover, Lawrence's imagery does not reach its climax until the final love scene, in which Constance becomes "a different woman" (297). On the other hand, the late story "The Woman Who Rode Away," which has some of the same disturbing tone and extremes as The

Plumed Serpent, satisfies us as a unified work of art. The extremes of heat and chill, which Lawrence carefully develops in the story, culminate in the epitomizing symbols of the sinking sun and the shaft of ice, which "was like a shadow between her and it" (*Complete Short Stories*, 2:580). In each of these later works, a pleasing integration of imagery and narrative results in a unity we may call organic. These same elements in *The Plumed Serpent*, without this integration, become merely mechanical.

Lawrence could scarcely write an uninteresting work. And certainly *The Plumed Serpent* is interesting throughout most of its first half and sporadically in its second half. But when Lawrence allows the central action to divorce itself from the controlling imagery, he loses the novel. If there is a lesson in this, it is that a novelist who works as extensively through a texture of imagery as Lawrence does can create a difficulty—and a danger—requiring intricate navigation. It may be that very often a novel's imagery is the nearly spontaneous development of the novelist's ideas or preoccupations. If so, it requires him to have good instincts. What may have happened in *The Plumed Serpent* is that Lawrence temporarily lost his good instincts, as happens to most novelists at one time or another. Lawrence's ill health and his frequent despondency (reflected in the *noli me tangere* sentiment of his protagonists of this period) had to be a distraction, as the plot's harsh and violent extravagances would appear to indicate. The shorter works of this time could more nearly resist the distractions that the longer work could not. Nonetheless, *The Plumed Serpent* bruises us into a sort of attention—not entirely in spite of its being a failure but in some small measure, at least, because it *is* a failure. About Lawrence's craft in particular, especially the light it sheds upon the virtues of his more successful works and about novel-writing in general, *The Plumed Serpent* still has things to teach us.

Chapter 7

The Virgin and the Gipsy
Insides and Outsides

A decision I faced in planning this study was whether to include a chapter on *The Virgin and the Gipsy*. That this novella was not published in Lawrence's lifetime counts for little: it is an almost totally successful, albeit minor, work. Knopf published it with the qualification that the manuscript lacked "the author's final revision."[1] Yet, in reading it, one wonders what changes Lawrence might have made. Almost everything seems right. This is Lawrence writing in the spare (for him), engagingly satiric manner of *The Captain's Doll*. The phrases, sentences, whether in service of character or landscape, are effortlessly effective. The rector, the Mater, and Cissie are each marvelously, mischievously, economically, captured. And Lawrence brings the bleak March Derbyshire setting into just enough focus to allow the broad symbolic scheme of the story to unfold.

The Virgin and the Gipsy interests Lawrencians for a number of good reasons. There is, of course, the mystery of why it was never published. Though a typescript had been prepared, Secker finally declined to print it. The question, then, is why Lawrence did not press on. I will offer a reason later. Second, the story is interesting as an anticipation of *Lady Chatterley's Lover*, as both Harry T. Moore in passing and Keith Cushman in much fuller detail have observed. Third, the characters and their situations reflect biographical aspects of situations involving Frieda, her daughters, and Ernest Weekley. Lawrence must have had a lot of fun—horrible though some of the circumstances are—doing the Reverend Arthur Saywell and the awful Mater and Cissie. A more than faint Dickensian aura hangs about the characterizations.

Thin though the novella is, it has a good deal of imagery, mainly of the symbolic (as opposed to the metaphorical) variety. Most obvious, of course, is the water symbolism. There is good water: the river, the flood (in its effects); and bad water: the "sewerage sort of life" of the vicarage. And there is frozen water: Major Eastwood has been "resurrected" from being buried for twenty hours under snow. There is flower imagery, chiefly the

---

1. Lawrence wrote the novel quickly, beginning in late 1925 or, more likely, writing all of it in January 1926. For details of its composition, see Keith Sagar, *D. H. Lawrence: A Calendar of His Works*, 149.

references to Yvette's mother, and to Yvette also, as a "pure white snow-flower" (6, 7, 8, and elsewhere). Animal imagery occurs frequently. Say-well is a rat (130, 132), Granny a toad (29–30 and elsewhere). The flood when it arrives is a "shaggy, tawny wavefront of water advancing like a wall of lions" (154–55). These images, to be sure, are convenient and fairly conventional, but their implications for the entire novel are considerably more profound and complex than they might at first appear. All the imagery, in fact, is carefully subordinated to an overall design and arrayed to strategically reinforce that design from within.

The Virgin and the Gipsy is about the insides and outsides of individuals and institutions. Through a series of conflicts pivoting upon freedom and "enslavement," belief and unbelief, sanity and insanity, appearance and reality, and death and rebirth, the central action becomes a process of discovering or disclosing what these insides and outsides are and what they mean. Like all of Lawrence's fiction, *The Virgin and the Gipsy* is a novel of reform, and the reform works in two directions: from within to without and from without to within.

To take the most obvious example, the flood, Yvette has already been warned by the old gipsy woman's dream to "be braver in your heart, and listen for the voice of the water" (146). These words encapsulate the two-fold lesson of the novel: that to escape death, to be reborn, one must be alert to what is both within oneself and without. When the flood comes, carrying all the cleansing violence of nature, it ransacks the unhealthy insides of the vicarage and kills the Mater, one of the two foremost symbols of the seweragelike inner life that has to be purged. But we observe that "the flood was in [Yvette's] soul" as well; thus, with the flood she becomes symbolically the killer of the obscene, toadlike Granny. It is finally the greater "bravery of the body" or "heart," that saves Yvette. "Not good enough: Not good enough!" the gipsy says of both the house and grandmother. A portion of the inside is good enough—the chimney, for instance. Critics usually conceive of the chimney in terms of phallicism and associate it with the gipsy. But the reader should consider also that the upstairs portion of the house that remains standing is Yvette's and may infer consequently that the chimney stands as much through its connection with Yvette's room as the room does from its being connected with the chimney. Yvette now is no longer imprisoned inside the rectory and the sort of suffocating institutionalized life it represents with its dedication to the observance of appearances. The inward changes, then, are complemented by the outward directions her life will take toward realities. It would not seem necessarily "a scaling down," as Cushman puts it,[2] for

---

2. Cushman, "The Virgin and the Gipsy and the Lady and the Gamekeeper," 165.

Yvette to discover the gipsy's name is Joe Boswell, her "obdt. servant" (175). My guess is, considering what has gone before, the gipsy's letter has a tinge of irony about it. And Yvette's learning he has a name is part of the journey outward. Gipsies, as well as the Leo Wetherells, have names, and though "Joe Boswell" is a commonplace name, so is "Oliver Mellors."

Lawrence makes the gipsy the inheritor of the pagan ethic. Though he establishes no direct link between the gipsy and Pan (who is never mentioned), the Pan-nature is present and active in the person of Joe Boswell. Most significantly, he is an "outlaw" in the broad, institutional sense of the word: "Being of a race that exists only to be harrying the *outskirts* of our society, forever hostile and living only by spoil, he was too much master to himself, and too wary, to expose himself openly to the vast and gruesome clutch of our law. He had been through the war. He had been enslaved against his will, that time" (142; my italics). He had been, in fact, Major Fawcett's groom, an "A.I. man with horses" (109) like Mellors, also a groomsman in the war. We may also link him with Dionys in *The Lady-bird*, who has the same wariness and whose last name, Psanek, means "outlaw." When he comes to the rectory the second time to sell his wares, Yvette from the window watches him "*outside* the white gate, with that air of silent and forever-unyielding *outsideness* which gave him his lonely, predative grace" (142; my italics). By contrast, Yvette "was born *inside* the pale" (143; my italics).

But he troubles Yvette because, unlike the others, he is the one person who knows her from the inside. She feels that when he looks at her it is "not from the outside, but from the inside, from her secret female self" (84). He has this ability because he exists outside the outside world of institutions, of "society," and inside the inside world of human emotions and sexuality. Yvette, on the other hand, who still lives within the social framework but whose instincts are nonetheless "to chip against the pillars of the temple, from the inside" (143), wonders why people seem like so many "mortal pieces of furniture" (84) and asks herself over and over, "Why is nothing important?" (85). What is becoming more important to her is the way that she is looked at. At the dance, bored and disillusioned, Yvette remembers the gipsy and his look: "the straight nose, the slender mobile lips, and the level, significant stare of the black eyes, which seemed to shoot her in some vital, undiscovered place, unerring" (90). It is interesting to compare Leo's look several pages later, after he has asked her to marry him: "But instead of penetrating into some deep, secret place, and shooting her there, Leo's bold and patent smile only hit her on the outside of the body, like a tennis ball, and caused the same kind of sudden irritated reaction" (93). Both passages make strategic use of sexual imagery: the first establishes the gipsy's phallic vitality (though the candlestick ten pages earlier with its "thick stem of copper, rising from a double bowl" does this nicely also); the second establishes the lack of vitality in Leo. He is all social gestures and games, of no more potency than a tennis ball. Sex with Leo would bounce off her, would induce only an "irritated reaction" (93). He has no insides from which either to look or make love. He is, in this respect, the secular counterpart of the rector.

The rectory is the symbol of the horrible (there *can* be a wonderful) inside life. The rector, the Mater, and Cissie are all "indoors" people. The central tension, of course, consists in whether the sisters, particularly Yvette, will themselves become indoors people or, like the gipsy, will free themselves to the outdoors life. (Though it may appear a bit too convenient and oversimplified, Lawrence himself expresses this idea with "indoors" and "outdoors.") Of the girls returning from their education abroad in France, Lawrence writes: "They were so terribly English. They seemed so free, and were as a matter of fact so tangled and tied up, *inside* themselves. They seemed so dashing and unconventional, and were really so conventional, so, as it were, shut up *indoors inside* themselves" (15–16; my italics). The freedom they have is really no freedom at all. They only "seem" to be "so free." Being "rudderless" (16) is little better than being its contrary, which is figured in the appalling house they arrive home to: "The rectory struck a chill to their hearts as they entered. It seemed ugly, and almost sordid, with the dank air of that middle-class, degenerated comfort which has ceased to be comfortable and had turned stuffy, unclean. The hard, stone house struck the girls as being unclean, they could not have said why. The shabby furniture seemed somehow sordid, nothing was fresh" (16). The house in fact "smelt of Granny" (21). But when Yvette opens the window to let the outdoors in, the rector immediately closes it again. The rectory quite simply is airless, lifeless. That contrast between the life of the rectory and that of the gipsy, whom Yvette has met on the outing to Bonsall, becomes increasingly clear to Yvette after the incident involving the church-window money and Aunt Cissie's "convulsion." Lawrence continues to play upon the contrast between inside and outside, the "sewerage sort of life" of the rectory versus the "fresh air" life of the gipsy's encampment. After the hurt Aunt Cissie's attack has done to her body, "in her sex," Yvette lies feeling "half-destroyed" and wishing "she were a gipsy" (61). She thinks, "To live in a camp, in a caravan, and never set foot in a house, not know the existence of a parish, never look at a church." We are told that she "loathed these houses with their indoor sanitation and their bath-rooms," where their "whole stagnant, sewerage sort of life, where sewer-age is never mentioned, but where it seems to smell from every two legged inmate, from Granny to the servants, was foul." By contrast, "If gipsies had no bathrooms, at least they had no sewerage. There was fresh air. In the rectory there was *never* fresh air" (61–62).

Lawrence's imagery here, as throughout, establishes a right and wrong kind of insides. With Yvette (and the gipsy) the concern is for the heart and "the sex"; with the rector and Granny, the digestive tract. Granny is described after meals as "perfectly complacent, sitting in her ancient obesity, . . . getting the wind from her stomach, pressing her bosom with her hand as she 'rifted' in gross physical complacency" (23–24). The rector, of course, is sexless—or rather is one who denies or frustrates sexuality. The girls' mother, "She-who-was-Cynthia," always had to be the "pure white snowflower." The double irony is that Saywell, though a minister of God, is without belief, a "life unbeliever" (59), as Yvette discovers: "Only dimly, after the row [over the money], Yvette began to realise the other sanctity of herself, the sanctity of her sensitive, clean flesh and blood, which the Saywells, with their so-called morality, succeeded in defiling" (58–59). Yvette's "fortune" as told by the gipsy woman, couched in an indoors-outdoors trope, indicates the part of the insides the Saywells wish to destroy: "There is a dark man who never lived in a house. He loves you. The other people are treading on your heart. They will tread on your heart till you think it is dead" (62). In *The Virgin and the Gipsy*, as in other Lawrence novels, especially *Lady Chatterley's Lover*, sex and the heart are almost synonymous. Though Yvette and Lucille talk about their sexlessness (Yvette says, "Perhaps we haven't really *got* any sex, to connect us with men"), Yvette realizes, that there was "some hidden part of herself which she denied" (118). This is sex, to be sure, which the gipsy will awaken in Yvette, but it is also the heart. The old gipsy woman predicts: "But the dark man will blow the one spark [in the stamped-upon heart] into fire again, good fire. You will see what good fire!" (62).

Throughout the novel, fire is figured within the inside-outside dimension. In the Saywell's house, fire is misused. The only good, hot fire is in the living room "because of course, here Granny reigned" (20); that is, because here her toadlike complacency, moral and otherwise, domineered. But of course it is not a good fire except in the sense of being hot. It actually is unhealthy: Yvette: "It's stifling! It's unbearable. No wonder we've all of us always got colds" (21). The unhealthiness comes from its being hoarded, as it were, not let out, warming no one but the family. By contrast, the gipsy's fire is outside. "Fire is everybody's" (112) the gipsy says to Mrs. Fawcett.

One of the most interesting images in this respect is the snowflower that describes both Yvette and her mother. It is, as we have seen, the rector's term of affection for his former wife. The term was Weekley's for Frieda, though I have not seen the connection with *The Virgin and the*

Gipsy remarked by anyone. In Frieda's "And the Fullness Thereof . . ." (in *The Memoirs and Correspondences*), the following passage involving Widmer (Weekley) and Paula (Frieda) occurs: "He took her in his arms, gently, tenderly, repressing his passion, so as not to frighten her. 'My snowflower,' he said. . . ."[3] Repressed passion leads either to corrupted passion or to its own death. In *The Virgin and the Gipsy*, the rector still maintains an absurd regard for the "disreputable woman who had betrayed" him: "For in the pure loftiness of the rector's heart still bloomed the pure white snowflower of his young bride" (6). But we know his heart to be cold and arid, a very rocky soil and inhospitable climate to someone who had resisted being a pure white snowflower in the first place. When the image is applied to Yvette, however, it undergoes an interesting development. In effect, Yvette will follow the same course as her mother in breaking *out* of, freeing herself from, the morally and otherwise enslaving confines of the rectory. When she makes her second visit to the gipsy's camp, alone this time, she falls under the gipsy's spell. Whether or not the episode is convincing or well done, Lawrence's imagery, I think, is effective in connecting up the novella's beginning and end. The gipsy is watching Yvette drink her coffee *by the fire*: "On her face was that tender look of sleep, which a nodding flower has when it is full out, like a mysterious early flower, she was full out, like a snowdrop which spreads its three white wings in a flight into the waking sleep of its brief blossoming. The waking sleep of her full-opened virginity, entranced like a snowdrop in the sunshine, was upon her" (102). One notes the "full out" of what had been in and is now in danger of going *full* in, like Aunt Cissie and her virginity, and one notes the "sun," the greatest of the "outdoor" fires. Furthermore, there is the clever conflation, through the imagery, of the sun and the gipsy. When he asks her if she wants to go in the caravan, Lawrence provides a still further elaboration of the metaphor, this one connecting with the climactic events at the end of the story: "The childlike, sleep-waking eyes of her moment of perfect virginity looked into his, unseeing. She was only aware of the dark, strange effluence of him bathing her limbs, washing her at last purely will-less. She was aware of *him*, as a dark, complete power" (102). The "strange effluence" is the sunshine he carries within him, but Lawrence renders the effect in terms of water imagery: "bathing her limbs, washing her." This conflation of both sets of imagery—fire and water—in "dark power" is a neat stroke indeed, serving Lawrence's purposes superbly.

In the contexts both of the way that Lawrence orchestrates his details—looking ahead, reaching back—and of his outside imagery, the trope of the flood advancing in "a shaggy, tawny wavefront . . . like a wall of

3. Frieda Lawrence, *The Memoirs and Correspondence*, 81.

lions" further evidences the comprehensive design and coherence of the novel. Two pages after this metaphor, we are told that the gipsy's "eyes glared on her like a tiger's" (157). Although it is clear that Lawrence is trying to connect the gipsy with the flood (both would destroy that which is not "good enough") without using the same animal image, the sentence might seem almost to come from the trash heap of melodramatic clichés, not worthy of Lawrence. It is important to see, though, that Lawrence's use of "lions" and "tigers" once again is part of a development, one that incorporates two other signally important symbolic images. In the first chapter, Lawrence writes of the Mater's hatred for the girls' mother, a hatred that carries over to the daughters: "This nettle actually contrived, at intervals, to get a little note through to her girls, her children. And at this the silver-haired Mater shook inwardly with hate. For if She-who-was-Cynthia ever came back, there wouldn't be much left of the Mater" (8). Yvette and Lucille remember quite distinctly "their real home, the Vicarage in the south, and their glamourous but not very dependable mother," who "made a great flow, a flow of life, like a swift and dangerous sun in the home" (8). Significant, of course, are the images of the "great flow, a flow of life" and the "swift and dangerous sun." They combine the same images Lawrence uses to describe the gipsy and his effect upon Yvette.

But Lawrence does not stop here: "Now the glamour was gone, and the white snowflower, like a porcelain wreath, froze on its grave. The danger of instability, the peculiarly *dangerous* sort of selfishness, like lions and tigers was also gone" (9). Every detail seems tailored for the conclusion. In terms of the novel's symbols, She-who-was-Cynthia does return (and we see the motive behind Lawrence's fusion of water and sun metaphors), making a very "great flow, a flow of life, like a swift and dangerous sun in the home." Indeed, afterwards there is not "much left of the Mater." The great destructive and simultaneously life-giving forces of nature, as Lawrence views them, (i.e., the great "outside world" of lions and tigers) sees to that. Only a healthy and living "insides" is proof against these forces yet is also capable of *receiving* from them. Such a complete person, to be sure, is "dangerous," is "insane" (the flood is described as "an insane sea of waters" [162]) in the daemonic sense. The rector, from his corrupt, institutionalized perspective, is perfectly correct in threatening Yvette with the "lunatic asylum. Exactly as if a distaste for Granny and for that horrible house of relatives was in itself a proof of lunacy, dangerous lunacy" (140). Being only unicorn is not good enough—the individual must be lion as well. The house, symbol of the world's idea of normalcy, is thus reduced to being practically all outsides, having been, but for the portion occupied by Yvette and the gipsy, effectively demolished by the flood. The following morning "the sun was shining in heaven," and the house seems grateful for its destruction: it "leaned forwards as if it were making a stiff bow to the stream" (167). Life has triumphed over death, belief over unbelief, sanity ultimately over insanity. Sun and water, or heart and body, have won. Along loosely mythic lines, we may say that nature has prevailed over the de-natured.

Yet, despite the fine orchestration of imagery, what *The Virgin and the Gipsy* lacks is precisely what the other longer fiction after *Aaron's Rod* has: density of detail, texture, subtexture. Images do engage one another, metaphors anticipate or "pick up" others, but Lawrence has not really submerged his imagery here as he has in the other later novels. We do not find the interpenetration of metaphor that we find in these other works. Rather, as in *The Captain's Doll*, Lawrence proceeds mainly on the level of symbol: the swollen river, the bursting dam. Moreover, we have only to contrast the gipsy with Mellors or with Dionys in The Ladybird, which is something less in length than *The Virgin and the Gipsy*, to see how thinly textured the latter novella is. We do not find quite the richness of mythic texture that is present in these other works.

The Virgin and the Gipsy, then, has something of importance to tell us about Lawrence's longer fiction after *Aaron's Rod*. In what is absent from it as well as what is there, it serves to document Lawrence's method in his last decade. From what we know, Lawrence wrote only one draft of the novella. We will see what happens through the successive drafts of *Lady Chatterley's Lover*.[4] But whether something more in the way of texture would have come from another draft of *The Virgin and the Gipsy* is not really the point. The point is that Lawrence's language in his later fiction requires and generously rewards close attention.

4. For a thorough treatment of Lawrence's revisions in the *Lady Chatterley* novels, see in particular Michael Squires, *The Creation of Lady Chatterley's Lover*.

Chapter 8

The Interpenetrating Metaphor
Nature and Myth in *Lady Chatterley's Lover*

While we obviously cannot take Oliver Mellors out of his woods (or the woods out of Mellors) in *Lady Chatterley's Lover* and have anything like the same book, we may still ask to what extent the novel's nature imagery, the purely descriptive or figurative language, serves Lawrence's purposes. That is, if we strip *Lady Chatterley* of its metaphors and similes, do we materially impoverish the whole? Does, for instance, a simile comparing the gamekeeper to a "lonely pistil in an invisible flower" (98) advance the action in any significant way? Certainly most of the figures have sexual references and thus add texture. But I wish to show that the nature-sex imagery provides considerably more than texture or, rather, that the texture it provides becomes inseparable from the meaning it creates.

We cannot, however, discuss Lawrence's orchestration of this imagery apart from the modes within which he was working, those of the pastoral and of myth and ritual. Oddly, only within the last fifteen years or so have scholars significantly addressed these elements in *Lady Chatterley*. Michael Squires, the first critic to do so at length, grounds his parallels on two notable studies of the pastoral form. First, he establishes the criteria by quoting from Walter R. Davis's *Map of Arcadia*: "The standard pastoral action consists then of disintegration in the turbulent outer circle, education in the pastoral circle, and rebirth at the sacred center." In *Lady Chatterley's Lover*, the turbulent outer ring is, of course, the modern mechanistic society epitomized by Clifford Chatterley's collieries; the pastoral circle is Wragby Wood; the sacred center is the pheasant hut. As further evidence that *Lady Chatterley* is a pastoral, Squires then cites E. R. Curtius's discussion of the *locus amoenus*, "a beautiful shaded natural site whose minimum ingredients comprise a tree (or several trees), meadow, and a spring or a brook." Similarly, Kingsley Widmer labels the novel a "modern pastoral": "The European conventions (in contrast to the American pastoral, which usually lacked the erotic dimensions) provide an idyllic and regenerative sacred place for loving, such as a grove or rural retreat, whose description carries pagan religious meanings." Widmer argues that Lawrence, by the time he wrote the final version of the novel, believed that the solution to the problems of the day was to "pastoralize" society. More recently, Dennis Jackson has demonstrated the significance of pagan myth and ritual in *Lady Chatterley*. Having shown that Lawrence read in Frazer on at least two occasions, Jackson identifies Mellors with the King of the Wood at Nemi (both guard an oak wood), as well as with the green George and other summer or fertility figures discussed in Frazer.[1]

Even if Lawrence had not been consciously working within a mode or tradition (and Lawrence would probably not have been shy about identifying any intended folk or literary antecedent for Mellors), the claim that he was actually doing so suffers no great damage. In fact, considering the traditions within which *Lady Chatterley's Lover* appears to fall, we can appreciate the parallels even more fully if they are unconscious or semiconscious. But Lawrence unquestionably recognized that his treatment of his material had mythic or ritualistic proportions. When near the end of this chapter we look at the changes Lawrence made in the second version of the novel (published as *John Thomas and Lady Jane*) to produce the final version, we will see a strategy that molds a distinctly ritualistic central action from scenes that originally had only a rough relation to ritual.

What I want to do here and earlier studies do not attempt is to assess the significance of the nature imagery for the narrative—that is, to consider how this imagery affects the total meaning. The figures of speech in the novel have a way of overlapping, of crossing boundaries, indeed of becoming at times cross-references taking us forward or backward from one scene or passage to another. They almost always make connections beyond themselves. These interpenetrating metaphors, as I shall call them, not only relate literal terms to figurative terms but also vegetable images to animal and (to a lesser extent) mineral images, as well as relating each of these to the process of sexual-spiritual rebirth at the heart of the novel. Unless Lawrence can convince us that Connie's sexual regeneration is also her spiritual regeneration, the novel collapses. Thus the wood, as a sacred place, must impart its religious properties to the sexual activities taking place there. This transfer occurs, I believe, largely through the overlapping or interpenetrating nature images that describe the sexual act. Lawrence always routes rebirth from disintegration to integration: this process involves connecting one faculty and another within the individual (in Lawrence essentially mind consciousness and blood consciousness), in addition to connecting the individual and nature. The metaphors in *Lady Chatterley's Lover*—linking bird, beast, and flower (and air, water, earth) with one another and with hero and heroine—organically emblematize both the sexual-spiritual union of Connie and Mellors and a similar union

---

1. Squires, "Pastoral Patterns and Pastoral Variants in *Lady Chatterley's Lover*," 129–46; Davis, *Map of Arcadia*, 38; Curtius, *European Literature and the Middle Ages*, 195; Widmer, "The Pertinence of Modern Pastoral: The Three Versions of *Lady Chatterley's Lover*," 304, 308; Jackson, "The 'Old Pagan Vision': Myth and Ritual in *Lady Chatterley's Lover*," 260–71.

(symbolized, for instance, by the flower-bedecking scene) between them and the sacred wood, which is in effect the "cosmos," to use Lawrence's term.

I

As we might expect, the wood being the major locus of the novel, the preponderance of imagery is vegetable: tree, leaf, flower. The wood exists in polar opposition to Tevershall pit and town, the secondary locus (together with Wragby Hall). About a third of the way into the novel, we observe Clifford taking on renewed energy and life from the so-called improvements he is to make in the operations of the colliery. That this resurgence is bogus we know because its source is not the living world but the decayed one coming "out of the coal, out of the pit." As if life could flow from death! "The very stale air of the colliery was better than oxygen to him" (126–27). By contrast, we watch Connie fumbling toward a new life a few pages later in the scene with the pheasant hens and their chicks. Although she is terrified as she attempts to feed them (appropriately so, since they bring her and Mellors together), she persists with the help of Mellors, who educates her out of her clumsiness and fear—as he later is to do in their sexual life. Along the way she comes to regard the fowl with a "sort of ecstacy." She thinks, "Life, life. Pure, sparky, fearless new life!" (133). After she and Mellors have made love for the first time (through the agency of the hens and baby chicks), we see him alone in the wood experiencing mixed emotions about being "connected . . . up again" (139). He thinks of the way the industrial world "would destroy the wood, and the bluebells [would] spring no more." He then considers her vulnerability, for "somewhere she was tender, tender with the tenderness of the growing hyacinths." Finally we are told that "his penis began to stir like a live bird" (141).

When we look at these ten or so pages, we discover a development that is either very lucky or else very carefully thought through—one or the other, but not both. From the dead coal and stale air of Clifford's world, we proceed by way of the pheasants to Connie and Mellors's lovemaking, from there to Mellors's imaging of Connie in a flower trope, and from there to the penis-bird simile, the progression connecting up the principal actions of these pages, from Connie's recognition of the "Pure, sparky, fearless new life" to the description of Lawrence's channel for this renewal as a "live bird." We remember Tommy Dukes's earlier remark about modern civilization. "It's all going down the bottomless *pit*, down the chasm. And believe me, the only bridge across the chasm will be the phallus" (85; my italics).

We see the way in which imagery interpenetrates imagery, action inter-penetrates action, creating an exceptional coherence. The next several pages develop similarly. On the following afternoon Connie goes again to the wood. In her body she feels "the huge heave of sap" in the massive trees and "their silent efforts to open their buds" (143). Later "the wood was silent, still and secret in the evening drizzle of rain, full of the mystery of eggs and half-open buds, half-unsheathed flowers. In the dimness of it all trees glistened naked and dark as if they had unclothed themselves, and the green things on earth seemed to hum with greenness" (144). The overt purpose of these passages is to suggest Connie's own unfolding into life, but they also catch up the previous interpenetrating action (and imagery) through the juxtaposition of egg and bud and the simile of disrobing. More-over, the reference to the sap rising in the tree recalls the scene in which Connie, viewing her body in the mirror, finds it to be disturbingly "greyish and sapless," with "pear-shaped breasts" that are "unripe" (80). It also embraces the passage in which Connie thinks of the way that Clifford turns everything into words, "sucking all the life-sap out of living things" (108). What has seemed to be a rather casual figure is in reality a further casting of the net of metaphor, a sinking of the image deep into the reader's con-sciousness.

The leaf and tree and flower metaphors function in much the same way. Clifford's conversation with Connie early in the book about her hav-ing a baby seems to her the next day "like dead leaves, crumpling up and turning to powder, meaning really nothing, blown away on any gust of wind. They were not the leafy words of an effectual life, young with energy and belonging to the tree. They were the hosts of fallen leaves of a life that is ineffectual" (56). The obvious comment here is that the leaves are dis-joined, having severed their connection with the vital source. They are like the coal: vegetation that was. In a later scene in which Clifford is again talking, reading Racine to Connie, Lawrence uses contrasting imagery to refer to her. Thinking of Mellors, "She was gone in her own soft rapture, like a forest soughing with the dim, glad moan of spring, moving into bud. . . . She was like a forest, like the dark, interlacing of the oakwood. . . . Meanwhile the birds of desire were asleep in the vast interlaced intri-cacy of her body" (163). Unlike the figures in the previous passages, these are all positive because they describe regeneration and growth and inte-gration. Moreover, the metaphor "the dark interlacing of the oakwood" interpenetrates with that of the "birds of desire" asleep in the body's "vast interlaced intricacy." These in turn enter the vast interlacing of metaphor that runs through the novel. The interlocking of fowl-plant metaphors, demonstrated again in the passage quoted above, is recurrent. Lawrence has already, for instance, compared his hero's penis to a bird. In a later trope this sacred member takes on a "small bud-like reticence and tender-ness" (208), and in a still later one Connie describes it as "tiny and soft like a little bud of life" (252). These are metamorphoses appropriate to a "god of the wood." The effect is ultimately that of a sort of music in which the images form the chords. These images blend over the course of the novel with phallic similes comparing Mellors to flowers (daffodils) and parts of flowers: "And the keeper, his thin, white body, like a lonely pistil in an invisible flower" (98). A page later Connie rests against a pine tree and thinks of its "curious life, elastic and powerful, rising up. The erect, alive thing, with its top in the sun" (99). Each successive image strikes its corres-pondences, so dense (like the trees) and intertwined are the figures.

If some images have their tops in the sun, their lower parts exist within the earth. The several root metaphors in the novel are fascinating and, in their manner of conferring meaning, perhaps the most strategic of all. Here is Connie, thinking of her situation with Clifford: "It was as if thousands and thousands of little roots and threads of consciousness in him and her had grown together in a tangled mass, till they could crowd no more, and the plant was dying." She is afraid "of how many of her roots, perhaps mortal ones, were tangled with [his]" (97). No Lawrencian char-acter, certainly, wants to get entangled in any way or "merged" with any-one, and Connie does well to be afraid of Clifford or anyone. A second root metaphor occurs about two-thirds of the way into the development of Con-nie and Mellors's relationship. It involves a bit of after-play to their love-making during the sequence in which Connie is said to have been "born a woman": "What a mystery! What a strange heavy weight of mystery that could be soft and heavy in one's hand! The roots, root of all that is lovely, the primeval root of all full beauty" (209). The reader here must make a connection. If Mellors's testes are the root, then the phallus must be the stalk or trunk. Again we recall Tommy Dukes's statement about the impor-tance of the phallus to the survival of civilization. We recall also the phallic descriptions of the trees. If Wragby Wood is the forest primeval, then, this decidedly phallic forest must have its testicular roots primeval.

This figure is not so facetious as it may sound. Indeed, it has a clear and linear logic, as does the further development of the same metaphor: "He's got his root in my soul, has that gentleman" (253). Mellors makes this remark during his next-to-last meeting with Connie. He is being playful, but he is also speaking, as he nearly always does, in his role as "the priest of love." We have just seen what the root of that gentleman is; now we learn the home, or source, of that root. As I stressed at the outset, the reader must be convinced that Connie's sexual development is her spir-itual one as well. The corollary to this statement is that her spiritual regen-eration depends on her sexual regeneration. Mellors's apparently offhand remark locating the genitalia within the geography of the soul signifies more than the casual reader might at first suspect.

To compare *Lady Chatterley* with other Lawrence novels is to appreciate the unique strategic function of the nature imagery here. Although Lawrence's reputation for describing nature is deservedly high, the general view is that *Lady Chatterley's Lover* marks a falling off. Harry T. Moore's criticism is probably representative: "Nature appears fairly frequently in *Lady Chatterley's Lover*, though not so effectively as in previous novels; if Lawrence's descriptive powers had been at their height when he was writing *Lady Chatterley*, it would have made a far more forceful book."[2] As Moore acknowledges, however, Lawrence could still write nature passages charged with color, as is evident from the nature descriptions generally in the late works. But we do not quite expect from *Lady Chatterley* the almost unearthly "nature" scenes that somehow came from his pen in *The Rainbow* and *Women in Love*. The confrontation between Ursula and the horses late in the first novel and the "Moony" episode in the second are scenes, one feels, that Lawrence could not have *not* written, scenes that his daimon wrote, so to speak, though this is not to deny the shaping hand its part. In contrast, *Lady Chatterley* offers a thoughtful subordination of nature to the structure of meaning, an orchestration of detail that is purely the achievement of sullen craft.

What have been symbols in previous Lawrence novels become metaphors here. When Ursula passes through the wood near Willey Water before encountering the horses in the meadow, the trees are symbolic, not metaphoric. In *Lady Chatterley's Lover* the trees are, of course, both. The "commemorating" cypresses of *Aaron's Rod* are symbols, as are the eagles in their dalliance and the lily:

> Happy lily, never to be saddled with an *idée fixe*, never to be in the grip of a monomania for happiness or love or fulfilment. It is not *laisser aller*. It is life-rootedness. It is being by oneself, life-living, like the much-mooted lily. One toils, one spins, one strives: just as the lily does. But like her, taking one's own life-way amidst everything, and taking one's own life-way alone. Love too. But there also, taking one's way alone, happily alone in all the wonders of communion, swept up on the winds, but never swept away from one's very self. Two eagles in mid-air, maybe, like Whitman's "Dalliance of Eagles." Two eagles in mid-air grappling, whirling, coming to their intensification of love-oneness there in mid-air. In mid-air the love consummation. But all the time each lifted on its own wings: each bearing itself up on its own wings at every moment of the mid-air love consummation. That is the splendid love-way. (*Aaron's Rod*, 166–67)

2. Harry T. Moore, *D. H. Lawrence: His Life and Works*, 246.

Here the eagles and the lily merely symbolize the ethic that Lilly embodies. Obviously, though, Lawrence also uses images metaphorically, as in this passage from *Aaron's Rod*:

> Sunlight, lovely full sunlight, lingered warm and still on the balcony. It caught the facade of the cathedral sideways, like the tips of a flower, and sideways lit up the stem of Giotto's tower, like a lily stem, or a long, lovely pale pink and white and green pistil of the lily of the cathedral. Florence, the flowery town. Firenze—Fiorenze—the flowery town: the red lilies. The Fiorentini, the flower-souled. Flowers with good roots in the mud and muck, as should be: and fearless blossoms in air, like the cathedral and the tower and the David. (232)

The lily figure serves the passage but, unlike the figures in *Lady Chatterley's Lover*, does not serve in any fully orchestrated way the central action of the story. It is primarily a mechanical component, not an organic one. We even find a metaphor within a metaphor, as in *Lady Chatterley*: "But I love it; it is delicate and rosy, and the dark stripes are as they should be, like the tiger marks on a pink lily. It's a lily, not a rose: a pinky white lily with dark tigery marks" (232). But the metaphors only feather, they do not interlock; we find no meshing of meaning, no engagement with prior or subsequent details. *Lady Chatterley* and *The Escaped Cock* are the mature achievements of the narrative technique that, as we have seen, had its beginnings in *Aaron's Rod*.

In the "Excurse" chapter of *Women in Love*, after Ursula and Birkin resolve their quarrel, Birkin is said to feel "as if he had just come awake, like a thing that is born, like a bird when it comes out of its egg, into a new universe" (312). At the inn they speak only through "the flowers in each other"; the strange passage in which Ursula kneels before Birkin incorporates river, flood, and fountain images. At the end of the chapter, they walk among "the great old trees" of Sherwood Forest, where, "like old priests," the fern rises in the distance, "magical and mysterious" (320). Like Mellors and Connie, Birkin and Ursula make love on the floor of the wood. But in this passage, unlike the one from *Lady Chatterley's Lover*, which I examine below, Lawrence provides no nature imagery at all. In short, although he gives us the vegetable, animal, and water imagery of previous parts of the chapter and endows the wood with a religious aura, we do not find any sort of organic interpenetration involving the images and the action. My point, of course, is not that there is anything amiss with his treatment of the scene here, or with his treatment of those in *Aaron's Rod*; it is simply that the absence of such a strategy in these novels and others points up the deliberate orchestration of the nature details in *Lady Chatterley's Lover*. What allows for it here, if not dictates it, is the blatantly phallic action. The orchestration is simply a matter of Lawrence's having found what suffices for him.

II

The nature imagery provides the texture for the main action of the novel. It is also the consequence of the action. Mellors is descended from the Green Man who figures prominently in both continental and British folklore—in the latter as the Jack-in-the-Green of holiday pageantry. Perhaps the most famous of Mellors's earlier manifestations is the Green Knight, Gawain's adversary and ultimate benefactor. When we first see Mellors, he is dressed in woodsman's green. He superintends the wood—a remnant of Sherwood Forest—and also the game within it, so that we identify him with both the animal and the vegetable spheres of the natural world. In the military he had served as a blacksmith with the cavalry. Clifford tells Connie that Mellors "always was connected with horses, a clever fellow that way" (106). He is responsible for the increase in the pheasants. (And of course he literally fertilizes Connie.) Yet, though we see him significantly in relation to animals (the dog Flossie, too, is usually at his side), it is in relation to the wood, in the general manner that Jackson describes, that he indeed becomes symbolic: he is the mythic fertility figure who will effect, along classical lines of ritualistic death and rebirth, Connie's regeneration.

Early in the novel, Lawrence contrasts the remnant of the wood with the chopped-down portion, which seems intended as a symbol of the war's destruction. He wants to show us the connections with an earlier time, that of Robin Hood and "of knights riding and ladies on palfreys": "The wood had some of the mystery of wild, old England. . . . How safely the birds flitted among [the] trees! And once there had been deer, and archers, and monks. . . . The place remembered, still remembered" (47). The last sentence contains an admonitory note; it suggests a vengeance to come. Connie is the observer here, walking Clifford in his chair. Then comes a remarkable passage, one of the two or three most important in the book. It establishes the novel's main action, the symbolic action, and looks ahead to its climax, the night of the "phallic hunt" at Mellors's cottage when Connie's sexual and spiritual development reaches its apotheosis:

> She was watching a brown spaniel that had run out of a side-path, and was looking toward them with lifted nose, making a soft, fluffy bark. A man with a gun strode swiftly, softly out after the dog, facing their way as if about to attack them; then stopped instead, saluted, and was turning down hill. It was only the new gamekeeper, but he had frightened Con-

nie, he seemed to emerge with such a swift menace. That was how she
had seen him, like the sudden rush of a threat out of nowhere. (51)

All students of twentieth-century literature will appreciate the implications
of the gun. But it is Mellors's bearing, his threatening aspect, that domi-
nates the other details of the passage. Not content to give us only one detail
that alarms Connie, Lawrence gives us several: Mellors faces the Chat-
terleys as if "to attack"; he emerges with "swift menace"; he is like a "sudden rush of a threat out of nowhere." He represents a direct challenge to
Clifford's way of life and Connie's sterile existence. Of course he frightens
her, for he is to be her executioner as well as her savior. She must die out of
her old existence before she can enter her new one—the old leaves must
fall before the new ones emerge: " 'Ye must be born again! I believe in the
resurrection of the body! Except a grain of wheat fall into the earth and die,
it shall by no means bring forth. When the crocus cometh forth I too will
emerge to see the sun.' In the wind of March endless phrases swept through
her consciousness" (98). As we shall see, Connie's "death" coincides with
her rebirth. This first encounter between Connie and the gamekeeper,
with its heavy symbolic quality, anticipates the travail of Connie's coming
through. A glance at the corresponding scene in the second version of the
novel, published in 1972 as *John Thomas and Lady Jane*, reveals a conscious shaping of strategy in the passage quoted above. The changes point
to Lawrence's effort to make the confrontation clearly symbolic:

> Out of the side riding came the gamekeeper, dressed in greenish
> velveteen corduroy. He looked at the two intruders, and touched his old
> brown hat in a salute, then was going on, evasive, down the hill, making
> a soft noise to call his dog. He was striding away.
> "Oh I say, Parkin!" said Sir Clifford.
> The man stopped and swung round suddenly, showing his red face
> and enquiring eyes, as if he expected some attack.
> "Sir?"
> "Turn my chair round for me, and get me started, will you? It makes
> it easier for me."
> Parkin came striding up the slope, with a quick small movement
> slinging his gun over his shoulder. He was a man of medium build. His
> face almost vermilion-ruddy with the weather wearing a rather sticking-
> out brown moustache. His bearing had a military erectness and resis-
> tance, that was natural to him, and at the same time he was silent, his
> movements were soft, silent, almost secretive or evasive. (*John Thomas
> and Lady Jane*, 27)

Though the gamekeeper (Parkin in this version) wears his green velveteen
and carries the gun, almost everything else about the scene is different.
Here he acts as if it were *he* who might be attacked, not the other way

around. There is nothing at all menacing or threatening about him. Despite his military posture, he seems more recessive than aggressive. The entire tone of the passage is different. In the *John Thomas* version the lady meets "his glance almost without knowing it" and "is hardly aware of him, being so much disturbed in herself by what Clifford had said" (72). Then the point of view shifts to Parkin, who feels "the queer spark of appeal touch him somewhere." But in *Lady Chatterley* we are told that "he stared straight into Connie's eyes, with a perfect, fearless, impersonal look" (52). The point of view stays with her, and it is she, we perceive, who is affected: he makes her feel "shy" and at the same time curious about him. In brief, the revisions transform the entire tenor of the scene and set up a second development. The meeting in *John Thomas and Lady Jane* sets up nothing.

A second important symbolic scene in *Lady Chatterley* occurs when Connie is returning from her visit to Mrs. Flint. She has made love to Mellors now on two occasions but, having become revolted by him, has avoided him for several days:

> Connie climbed the fence into the narrow path between the dense, bristling young firs. Mrs. Flint went running back across the pasture, in a sunbonnet, because she was really a school teacher. Constance didn't like this dense new part of the wood; it seemed grotesque and choking. She hurried on with her head down, thinking of the Flints' baby. It was a dear little thing, but it would be a bit bow-legged like its father. It showed already, but perhaps it would grow out of it. How warm and fulfilling somehow to have a baby, and how Mrs. Flint had showed it off! She had something anyhow that Connie hadn't got, and apparently couldn't have. Yes, Mrs. Flint had flaunted her motherhood. And Connie had been just a little bit jealous. She couldn't help it.
>
> She started out of her muse, and gave a little cry of fear. A man was there.
>
> It was the keeper; he stood in the path like Balaam's ass, barring her way. (155–56)

Indeed, she is in a deeper part of the forest, quite literally and figuratively. Disturbed, since she is still trying to avoid Mellors, she seeks only an exit. But there he is, suddenly, barring her way. By force of his will he leads her "into the dense fir trees, that were young and not more than half-grown" (157). As the imagery suggests, Connie is in an intermediate stage of her growth. Then: "He led her through the wall of prickly trees, that were difficult to come through, to a place where was a little space and a pile of dead boughs. He threw one or two dry ones down, put his coat and waistcoat over them, and she had to lie down there under the boughs of the tree, like an animal" (157). With another author one might not be inclined to make anything of "prickly," but with Lawrence, in this context, the reader has every reason to consider it a phallic pun. The wordplay here is a strategic inversion of the interpenetrating metaphors considered previously, in which the figurative term is natural, the literal term sexual. That Connie is forced to "lie down . . . like an animal" signifies the animality of the act in which she is about to participate: her placement is part of her instruction. But the interpenetrating metaphors of the next paragraph make it clear that, though the act is an animal one, it connects the participant to the great world around her. Connie feels "new strange trills rippling inside her . . . like a flapping overlapping of soft flames . . . melting her all molten inside" (157). The fire and thermal imagery yields to sea imagery when her womb becomes "open and soft . . . like a sea anemone under the tide." Then a familiar vegetable image merges with the marine imagery to dramatize metaphorically the enlarging and interpenetrating character of Connie's experience:

> She clung to him unconscious in passion, and he never quite slipped from her, and she felt the soft bud of him within her stirring, and strange rhythms flushing up into her with a strange rhythmic growing motion, swelling and swelling till it filled all her cleaving consciousness, and then began again the unspeakable motion that was not really motion, but pure deepening whirlpools of sensation swirling deeper and deeper through all her tissue and consciousness, till she was one perfect concentric fluid of feeling. (158)

The largely mineral imagery here interacts with the other imagery to create a meaning beneath the surface of the action—a meaning that parallels the action and dramatically reinforces it. (The vitalistic language, moreover, mirrors an outcome of the scene, suggesting that Connie conceives during the act.) Connie's development is now two-thirds complete. The world has become vital around her. Smaller doubts may persist, but the large one is overcome. As Connie returns to Wragby Hall after a subsequent rendezvous with Mellors, the park trees, in another interpenetrating trope, "seemed bulging and surging at anchor on a tide, and the heave of the slope to the house was alive" (213).

If we look at what happens in *John Thomas and Lady Jane* we can once again find some instructive differences. Neither "prickly" nor "half-grown" appears in the earlier version, and Connie is not forced to lie "waiting like an animal." As we have seen, these additions to the scene in *Lady Chatterley* are key details within the novel's ritualistic dimensions. The most extensive revisions, though, are in the description of Connie and Mellors's copulation and Connie's orgasm. Here is Lawrence's earlier version:

> And then, something awoke in her. Strange, thrilling sensation, that she had never known before woke up where he was within her, in wild

thrills like wild, wild bells. It was wonderful, wonderful, and she clung to him uttering in complete unconsciousness strange, wild, inarticulate little cries, that he heard within himself with curious satisfaction.

But it was over too soon, too soon! She clung to him in a sort of fear, lest he should draw away from her. She could not bear it if he should draw away from her. It would be too, too soon lost. He, however, lay quite still, and she clung to him with unrelaxing power, pressing herself against him.

Till he came into her again, and the thrills woke up once more, wilder and wilder, like bells ringing pealing faster and faster, to a climax, to an ecstasy, an orgasm, when everything within her turned fluid, and her life seemed to sway like liquid in a bowl, swaying to quiescence. (127)

We find only three similes, two of them identical. Only one ("her life . . . like liquid in a bowl") is based on nature, and then only partially. By contrast, the description in *Lady Chatterley's Lover* mingles music, fire, bird, sea, and plant metaphors, overlapping and interlocking them. Note, for example, the remarkable layering of three metaphors in "trill . . . like a flapping overlapping of soft flames, soft as feathers." The most unobtrusive yet signally significant of the additions to the final version, however, is this paragraph:

But he drew away at last, and kissed her and covered her over, and began to cover himself. She lay looking up to the boughs of the tree, unable as yet to move. He stood and fastened up his breeches, looking round. All was dense and silent, save for the awed dog that lay with its paws against its nose. He sat down again on the brushwood and took Connie's hand in silence. (158)

The trancelike state of the surroundings conveys the symbolic magnitude of the scene. Even Flossie is "awed" by the magic and mystery of what has taken place. The mesmeric effect on her, in conjunction with the rest of the passage, nicely suggests the ritualistic aspect of the drama that has just transpired.

The account of the last stage of Connie's rebirth, which takes place at Mellors's cottage, involves mainly fire imagery, consistent with Mellors's purging from Connie the "deepest, oldest shames" (297), and mineral imagery ("smelt out the heaviest ore of the body to purity"; "the real bed-rock of her nature" [297–98]). We can now understand why Lawrence described Mellors's initial appearance as threatening, menacing in all aspects. As Green Man (whose modus operandi in this scene may have more of the

Greek than the English in it),[3] he must hunt out and kill in order to purify, must destroy in order to resurrect. Connie "really thought she was dying: yet a poignant, marvelous death." The victim, the prey, is Connie's "shame": the "deep organic shame . . . which crouches in the bodily roots of us, and can only be chased away by the sensual fire, [and] at last it was roused up and routed by the phallic hunt of the man, and she came to the very heart of the jungle of herself" (98). The reader observes the presence once more of "roots" and the apt deepening of the metaphor into "jungle" (from forest). And Mellors afterward is "like a wild animal asleep." If these metaphors do not immediately blend like those in earlier passages, there is nonetheless an interplay, a resonance. The success of the scene may not depend on the interlacing of the imagery between this passage and previous ones, but it certainly builds on these connections.

In *Lady Chatterley*, Lawrence devotes eight paragraphs to a scene that requires only four in the *John Thomas* version, for he now clearly intends the scene to be the climax of Connie's education. We can see what he left out in the earlier version by looking at its two middle paragraphs:

> Now, however, after this night, she knew it meant stages of sensual intensity, and degrees of refinement in the different practices of sensuality. In this one short summer night, a new range of experience opened out to her, frightening, but acute as fire, and necessary. She had never known it was necessary, till she had it. And now at last she felt she was approaching the real bed-rock of her nature, her intrepid sensual self. She thought she would have been ashamed. But she was not ashamed. She felt a triumph, almost a vainglory. So that was what one was! That was it! There was no more to suppress.
>
> But what a reckless devil the man was! One had to be strong to bear him! She felt that she was mated. And that was what had been at the bottom of her soul all the time! the hunger for the daredevil, sensual mate! What liars poets were! at least for her. Communion of love, and all the rest! When the bed-rock was sharp, flamey, rather awful sensuality. And the man who dared do it, without shame or sin or abating his pride. If he had been shamed, it would have been awful. But now, in the morning light, he slept with the innocence and also the mystery of the full sensual creature. As a tiger sleeps with its ears half pricked. (271)

3. Clifford Chatterley in fact speaks, after the manner of Cellini, of "the Italian way" in describing, according to Bertha Coutts, Mellors' sexual use of Connie (322). Whether Mellors had anal intercourse with Connie was of course the subject of the famous controversy beginning in 1961 in *Encounter* and concluding finally in 1963 in *Essays in Criticism*. In the back pages of the latter journal, John Peter, contending that Mellors did not have anal intercourse with Connie, took on such formidable opponents as G. Wilson Knight and William Empson. An impartial reader would allow that Peter was routed.

We find no mention of the phallic hunt, no intensification of forest to "jungle." The *John Thomas* version does refer to the purging of Lady Jane's "shame," but only as a side issue. In *Lady Chatterley* the scene focuses on this theme:

> In the short summer night she learnt so much. She would have thought a woman would have died of shame. Instead of which, the shame died. Shame, which is fear: the deep organic shame, the old, old physical fear which crouches in the bodily roots of us, and can only be chased away by the sensual fire, at last it was roused up and routed by the phallic hunt of the man, and she came to the very heart of the jungle of herself. She felt, now, she had come to the real bed-rock of her nature, and was essentially shameless. She was her sensual self, naked and unashamed. She felt a triumph, almost a vainglory. So! That was how it was! That was life! That was how oneself really was! There was nothing left to disguise or be ashamed of. She shared her ultimate nakedness with a man, another being.
>
> And what a reckless devil the man was! really like a devil! One had to be strong to bear him. But it took some getting at, the core of the physical jungle, the last and deepest recess of organic shame. The phallus alone could explore it. And how he had pressed it on her!
>
> And how, in fear, she had hated it. But how she had really wanted it! She knew now. At the bottom of her soul, fundamentally, she had needed this phallic hunting out. (298)

What we see is both a concentration and an expansion of the same material. We have the satisfying sense, missing in the Ur-passage, that this scene is the culmination of a significant symbolic action. The change from "In the short summer night she had learnt so much" to "she had needed this phallic hunting out" reveals the central meaning of the novel in its final development: the phallic education of Constance Chatterley through the primitive green agency of her husband's gamekeeper.

This episode consummates, then, the major action of the novel. The rest, approximately a quarter of the whole, is denouement. Her rebirth or resurrection accomplished, Connie no longer requires the sacred wood, and the novel suffers as a result: what follows contains a good bit of Lawrencian silliness. Lawrence is at his best in the episodes set in Wragby Wood, in those scenes focused squarely on Connie's fruition. He is at his worst, his most artificial, when he allows a secondary character, moreover one whom we are intended to dislike—Tommy Dukes in the first part of the book, Connie's father in the last—to mouth certain of his ideas. The same is true of Mellors when he forgets that he is a Green Man of (symbolic) action and fancies himself the polemicist. Even Connie can be insufferable once she participates in Mellors's views and her voice becomes indistinguishable from his, as it does at times in the last quarter of the book. But in showing her development, Lawrence is near the top of his form. It is unfortunate that Connie could not always remain "becoming."

One may well wonder why Lawrence felt the need to argue his point at all, having dramatized it to such superb effect in what is the true ending of the novel, that final, ritual love scene. Perhaps he felt disposed to contend further for his views since he had not worked out his own shame. I seriously doubt, however, that he had any reservations about his sexual ethic. It may be his literary instincts simply failed him here. At any rate, the scenes of Connie's awakening constitute the real, imaginative world of the novel. As we have seen, the metaphorical language of those episodes, through the interpenetrating action of the figures, overarches the central action, reinforcing and dramatizing Connie's sexual awakening and its fructifying consequences—the integration of the self and the vital connection with another individual and with the cosmos. The interaction of the images within the metaphorical structure of the novel is organic in that it reproduces, even creates, the effective meaning of *Lady Chatterley's Lover*. And this is no petty function.

Chapter 9

The Escaped Cock
The Imagery of Integration

Though *The Escaped Cock* (less expressively, *The Man Who Died*) is not major in the way that the great full-length novels are, it may be the most nearly perfect of them all. The first and second parts were written roughly a year apart, sandwiching drafts of *Lady Chatterley's Lover*. But there is no seam, as there are seams, say, in *Mr. Noon* and *Aaron's Rod*, two works whose composition was also interrupted. Lawrence's skill in reinforcing the action of *Lady Chatterley's Lover* with imagery so that the description ceases to be distinct from narration continues undiminished in *The Escaped Cock*. Few authors in similar circumstances have written fiction as well as the dying Lawrence did here. No author, it is safe to say, in his last years, wrote fiction, poetry (the wonderful "Bavarian Gentians" and "The Ship of Death"), and nonfiction prose (*Apocalypse*) that comes close to matching Lawrence. If *The Plumed Serpent* illustrates how a work's texture and action can get fatally out of synchronization, *The Escaped Cock* shows how these can be supremely right. Keith Sagar puts it nicely: "'The Escaped Cock' is written in a clear, fresh prose which does not assume its own inability to convince without a drumbeat and a plethora of images. The prose is poised and self-sufficient and implies a creating imagination similarly at one with itself and its material."[1] The point, I think, is significant. Having put away the unassimilable excesses of *The Plumed Serpent*, Lawrence could now give himself to the assimilable ones of *Lady's Chatterley's Lover* and *The Escaped Cock*. Sagar is wrong about the imagery, however, on one count. By the square inch there is at least as much imagery in *The Escaped Cock* as in any of the other fictions. It is just that the work has also assimilated the description so cunningly that we are not aware of how intensive or comprehensive it is.

It may be for this reason that though many critics (and reviewers earlier) have noted the beauty of the language and though many have written about the story's "meanings" and its place in the development of Lawrence's ideas, few have really discussed the language of the story in relation to its meaning. In short, few have discussed the *art* of the story. Harry T. Moore, for instance, remarks that the story is "Lawrence at his finest"

1. Sagar, *D. H. Lawrence: Life into Art*, 224–25.

and praises Lawrence's ability to "bring his setting vividly to life" but offers nothing in the way of showing how Lawrence does this. Although his title, *The Art of D. H. Lawrence*, promises more, Keith Sagar does not actually address the issue of this story's art except to compare favorably some of its rhythms to those in *The Plumed Serpent*. Without dealing with the language per se, two perceptive studies do examine in detail at least some of the story's symbols. Larry V. LeDoux looks at the symbolism conjunctive with the myth of the dying and reviving god, and James C. Cowan examines especially the symbol of the sun. The focus of neither study, however, is upon Lawrence's art. Closer to this task is Robert H. MacDonald's examination of the imagery of the story. MacDonald argues convincingly that the story is built upon the symbols and makes the extremely useful point that Lawrence works inventively through "constant comparison and juxtaposition" of images and through "repeated use of the same symbolic imagery."[2] While MacDonald focuses upon the symbols of fire and water and upon the thematic dimensions of the story, this chapter will show, in the way of preceding ones, the total artistic integration of language and meaning in the work.

I

The central tension in *The Escaped Cock* from which the imagery stems—and stems as a *live* metaphor because the imagery is vitally organic—is that between the "little day" of the "daily" people and "the greater day of the human consciousness" (*Escaped Cock*, 44). Two related thematic developments occur in the story. The first involves the man's progress out of dailiness into the larger life that is consummated in his sexual relations with the priestess of Isis. The second development involves the same agencies but requires a slightly different formulation: "Risen from the dead, he had realized at last that the body, too, has its little life, and beyond that, the greater life" (28). Through touch, the body, alive now with the man's recognition of having asked his followers to serve him with "the corpse of their love" and of having offered them only "the corpse of [his] own" (55), enters into relation with all the natural universe. The theme is the familiar one of the integration of the individual's "faculties" and of the vital connection of individual with another individual and with the "cosmos." Law-

---

2. Moore, *D. H. Lawrence: His Life and Works*, 249, 250; LeDoux, "Christ and Isis: The Function of the Dying and Reviving God in *The Man Who Died*; Cowan, *D. H. Lawrence's American Journey: A Study in Literature and Myth*; MacDonald, "The Union of Fire and Water: An Examination of the Imagery of *The Man Who Died*, 35, 40.

rence establishes these connections for the reader largely through imagery. This imagery grows, or expands, as the man, progressively sloughing off the spiritual-intellectual aridity of his previous "life," begins to grow in awareness of the emotions and the body. As his awareness embraces larger and larger worlds, the imagery embraces wider and wider categories, extending from organic to inorganic, from terrestrial and solar to cosmic, interfolding these categories so that they become an integrated, natural whole.

This imagery commences in the very first sentence: "There was a peasant near Jerusalem who acquired a young gamecock which looked a shabby little thing, but which put on brave feathers as spring advanced, and was resplendent with an arched and orange neck, by the time the fig-trees were letting out leaves from their end-tips" (13). The economy with which this sentence projects the central theme, initiating the imagery and through (implicit, for now) analogy establishing the basic situation, is masterly. The gamecock will be inspirational for the man because like the cock, the man himself is a "shabby little thing." But he too will put on his own "brave feathers." "Brave" in one sense hides its meaning, here suggesting color and vigor more nearly than courage, its usual meaning. But it intimates this meaning, which is important for the story, since courage, together with "wits" (60), is essential to living free and apart from a world that wishes to keep one on its leash. Most important of all, though, is the connection between the cock's putting out new feathers and the fig tree's putting out new leaves. In making the two coincident within the regenerative process of spring, Lawrence establishes the organic relation that holds among all life in the natural world.

A few pages later the connection is carried further. As the man, out of the tomb, proceeds into "the world, the same as ever, the natural world, thronging with greenness, a nightingale winsomely, wistfully, coaxingly calling from the bushes beside a runnel of water, in the world, the natural world of morning and evening, forever undying, from which he had died," he comes upon the "wild" crowing of the cock, which has just escaped its master. From the bough of an olive tree, it appears to him "leaping out of greenness," the feathers of his tail "streaming lustrous" (17). In the first passage the images of the cock and the tree (or the spring's green) were juxtaposed. But here these are united in a single image: "leaping out of greenness." The man, however, is still apart. Lawrence develops his imagery according to a design of progressive relationship from exclusiveness to inclusiveness, and from one or two to several, to many, to a complex. The imagery serves to indicate a fuller and richer meaning of the title by it taking the reader beyond the narrower Christian implication to the broader and—as the story pursues its implication—more important one. The man has died not merely from the world. He has died from the *natural* world. Lawrence has inserted into the middle of the preceding passage a nightingale, "winsomely, wistfully, coaxingly calling from the bushes beside a runnel of water" (17)—a subtle congregation of images, but all of them images of life (bird, bush, water) coaxing and calling the man from his willed division from them. As the man follows the peasant back to his cottage, feeling "the young green wheat under his feet that had been dead,"[3] the imagery accents this division: "At the edges of rocks he saw the silky, silvery-haired buds of the scarlet anemone bending downwards; and they too were in another world. In his own world he was alone, utterly alone. These things around him were in a world that had never died. But he himself had died . . . and all that remained now was the great void nausea of utter disillusion" (18). "These things" embrace the inorganic rocks as well as the organic anemone, anticipating a trope absolutely integral to the story's climactic scene.

Lawrence's method here is to spring image out of image, interpenetrating them as he does in *Lady Chatterley's Lover*. Thus, lying in the peasant's garden in the sun, the man watches "the first green leaves spurting like flames from the ends of the enclosed fig-tree" (20). The simile may appear no more than a local, conventional detail. Lawrence, however, is setting up a more elaborate figure and advancing an important thematic development. In the morning the man likes to lie in the sun, which was "the one thing that drew him and swayed him." Hearing the tethered cock crow its "brave sounds," he sees "a vast resoluteness everywhere flinging itself up in stormy or subtle wave-crests, foam-tips emerging out of the blue invisible, a black-and-orange cock, or the green flame tongues out of the extremes of the fig-tree." They come, all of them, "like crests of foam." Watching the cock feed, the man sees "not the bird alone, but the short, sharp wave of life of which the bird was the crest" (21). Lawrence, of course, wants to assert that both sets of images, wave and flame, have a similar source, nature, and more concretely, that they are synecdoches of the two great sources of life, the sea and the sun. Each image connects with, interpenetrates, another: e. g., the "green flame tongues" appear "like crests of foam." Above all, however, in preparation for the central action of the story involving the man and the priestess of Isis, Lawrence wants to assert the sexuality of this spring. When he describes life as "a short, sharp wave" with the cock as "the crest," he is describing its overwhelmingly phallic

3. MacDonald makes more of the wheat than I would: "Lawrence uses too the symbols of the traditional myths, the green wheat of Osiris, the sun of Osiris and Christ, the moon of the goddess Isis" ("Fire and Water," 36). Though its presence gives texture, the wheat (and the moon, for that matter) does not seem to me significantly enough developed to warrant equal status with the sun in this statement.

aspect. When the cock mounts, minutes later, his favorite hen, the man watches not the birds, "but one wave-tip of life overlapping for a minute another, in the tide of the swaying ocean of life" (22). It is difficult to determine whether Lawrence is portraying life in terms of the sexual, or the sexual in terms of life. It would seem the latter, since the man looks beyond the literal physical act of copulation to the act described through images connoting life (water, the ocean). But the imagery itself is phallic ("wave-tip," already associated with "flame tongue"). It is interesting that Lawrence describes the more concrete thing (sexual act) in terms of the more general (life), reversing the usual procedure—and motive—of metaphor. The point, I think, is that Lawrence wants us to see that they are indivisible. In the same way, "green jets of leaves unspread on the fig-tree, with the bright, translucent green blood of the tree" (30). The leaves, of course, are no more "jets," or flames, than the sap of a tree is blood. They are of a different order. But their difference is less apparent than their similarity. Lawrence would have us see the interpenetration of all things that live and give life: Animal and vegetable do not exist apart from each other or from the sun that gives life to both. The image, with its reference to blood, followed by the description of the cock's growing brighter, day by day "more lustrous with the sun's burnishing," advances the meaning and looks forward to the full, phallic dimension of Part Two. Though the "old nausea" (34) is in the man as he sets forth on his quest to find the woman who can "lure my risen body, yet leave me my aloneness" (32), he has the example of the sun-burnished cock, which has just defeated the "common" cock of the innkeeper's yard, to lead him through the "compulsions" and "mean contacts" of the common, fearful, and bullying world that would "violate his intrinsic solitude" (34).

II

For Lawrence, the two conditions necessary to an authentic existence are personal intactness on the one hand and integration with the natural world on the other. The preferred way to that integration is through a phallic relationship. The difficulty, from the time of *Sons and Lovers* on, is that the woman who could complete the phallic relationship often wants more of the man than Lawrence, or his protagonist, was willing to give her. All of Lawrence's major works revolve around this problem (though sometimes the situation, as in *St. Mawr*, is reversed). It is not, of course, only women who represent a threat to a man's isolation. The daily world at large represents a similar threat, as seen above. In either instance, envy or resentment of wholeness causes either the woman or the world of men to seek to undermine or crack this wholeness. Of Lawrence's novels after *Women in Love*, only in the last two do we find (for the characters themselves) mainly satisfactory resolutions. The reason behind this late development lies largely in the fact, I think, that Lawrence, dying, was seeking satisfying resolutions. That *Lady Chatterley* is in good measure a fairy tale and *The Escaped Cock* a fantasy of sorts detracts little from their considerable merits. It is significant that at the end Lawrence causes the man, fulfilled in his quest, to leave the priestess, as if any sustained relation would threaten his isolation. At any rate, the imagery sustains both of the overriding thematic developments.

At the beginning of the second part, for instance, two pairs of images pick up and carry over the two central themes of the first part. In one pair of images, the olive trees of the Levant are described as being "silvered under the wind like water splashing" (35). The portrayal of one nature image in terms of a second from another category conveys a sense of the interrelatedness of vegetation and sea (and wind). The second pair of images more comprehensively establishes the connection and renders the insistent theme of isolate integrity: "Upon it all poured the royal sunshine of the January afternoon. Or rather, all was part of the great sun, glow and substance and immaculate loneliness of the sea, the pure brightness" (36). Although the sea takes in the sun and glows from it, it retains its essential private character, or exclusiveness. It is part and apart, which is the condition the man seeks. The primary image, though, in Part Two, is the sun. Appropriately enough given Lawrence's advocacy of "natural aristocracy," the sun radiates "royal" sunshine. It is a decidedly phallic natural aristocrat, too: "And in the winter afternoon the light stood erect and magnificent off the invisible sea, filling the hills of the coast" (35). At this moment the priestess of Isis stands looking down from her temple to the shore; the man arrives to witness with her the slave boy's hasty and rather brutal taking of the slave girl. The juxtaposition of image and episode is hardly accidental. The image, moreover, anticipates the climactic scene in the priestess' temple. The full extent to which Lawrence has thought through his imagery, orchestrated it, will become clear at that point. Suffice it to say for now that, "spontaneously" as Lawrence wrote, it appears a spontaneity under remarkable internal control, particularly in light of its accuracy and arrangement.

In this second part the sun is the featured image, along with the flower, whose female sexual properties, of course, complement the sun's male ones. Whether lotus, or rose, or even crocus, the flower is the necessary completing part of the process or complex of imagery that begins with the sun. The Isis that the priestess serves is the "Isis in Search"; that is, in search of the fragments of Osiris, "dead and scattered asunder, dead, torn apart, and thrown in fragments over the wide world." Now, having found the fragments and assembled them, she seeks the "last reality" that will truly reunite him to her: "For she was Isis of the subtle lotus, the womb which waits submerged and in bud, waits for the touch of that other, inward sun that streams its rays from the loins of the male Osiris" (38). The priestess, whose father had been a captain in Mark Antony's army, had herself been the object of Antony's seductive endearments featuring the same images: "Come, why is the flower of you so cool within? Does never a ray nor a glance find its way through? Ah come, a maid should open her bud to the sun, when the sun leans towards her to caress her." Because her "bud" remains cool and is later cool toward other men, she inquires about love of a "philosopher," who tells her that "Rare women wait for the reborn man. For the lotus, as you know, will not answer to all the bright heat of the sun. But she curves her dark, hidden head in the depths, and stirs not" (39). It is only when, at night, "one of those rare, invisible suns that have been killed and shine no more, rises among the stars in unseen purple, and like the violet, sends its rare, purple rays out into the night" that the lotus "offers her soft, gold depth such as no other flower possesses, to the penetration of the flooding, violet-dark sun that has died and risen and makes no show" (39–40). This is imagery that draws attention to itself as imagery and, in my view, though effective enough in sending along the central idea of phallic love, is not on the same level as imagery that blends itself into the subtext or undermeaning of the story. *The Ladybird* is a better handling of the "dark sun" concept, and both *Kangaroo* and *Lady Chatterley's Lover* advance much more effectively the characterization of a hero ("invisible sun") who has been somehow killed at the center of his being, who makes no more "show," but who yet has the tenacity and vitality to "rise" in the struggle toward the familiar Lawrencian ideals. Fortunately, Lawrence rises above this passage when he has to in the novel's crucial episode.

He also exceeds it in many of those seemingly isolated figures that nonetheless fold themselves into the texture I spoke of above. These figures resonate a deeper tone to complement the necessary "deeper life" (43) that the story finally is about. When the priestess, the first time, bids the man see her, we are told that "he went slowly, staying to look at the pale-blue sea like a flower in unruffled bloom" (44). Though the figure is hardly spectacular, it dexterously connects the man and the woman with the images that describe them: the sea, in its loneliness, and the flower, in its womblike receptivity. The joining of the two images anticipates, moreover, the sexual union of the man and the priestess. When he leaves, he walks down to the shore and reflects: "I am a physician, yet I have no healing like the flame of this tender girl. The flame of this tender girl! Like the first pale crocus of the spring. How could I have been blind to the healing and the bliss in the crocus-like body of a tender woman! Ah tenderness!" (46). The flame, described through the further metaphor of the crocus, links images in the manner of those we have observed in Part One. The most interesting touch, though, is the man's then prizing shellfish from the rocks and eating them "with relish and wonder for the simple taste of the sea." The combining of this action and the crocus metaphor, together with the metaphor of the sea blooming like a flower, frames the first meeting of the man and priestess with images that are organic constructs of the scene itself. The effect is wonderful, almost subliminal. The reader, consciously, can hardly be aware of what has occurred in the way that, consciously, he has to be aware of the sun-lotus figure. They work entirely on different levels of awareness. The subtextual insinuation of meaning, which is the triumph of the best of the later work, is the triumph of *The Escaped Cock*.

The imagery of the climactic last part of the story is of both varieties described above, but even when it is of the second sort it carries forward or reinforces previous images and developments. When the man, having put aside his fears, goes to the priestess in the temple, he thinks of her "strange difference" from him: "What a beautiful thing, like the heart of a rose, like the core of a flame. She is making herself completely penetrable" (53). These images of tenderness and passion, fused here, catch up the images in Part One of flower and "jet." But now they have grown, have taken up residence, as it were, within the central action itself. Other images, exfoliating from previous ones, follow. In each there is an advance. After rubbing the man's body with oil, she embraces him so that her breasts are in the wounds in his sides and presses "him to her, in a power of living warmth, like in the folds of a river." It is a sort of baptism for him, a submersion, signifying the rebirth, or "dawn," the "new sun . . . coming up in him, in the perfect inner darkness of himself" (56). When he caresses her then, he thinks of her in terms of what seems at first a wholly unlikely image, a rock. "He knew only the crouching fulness of the woman there, the soft white rock," the rock on which, as he says now, "'I build my life.' The deep-folded, penetrable rock of the living woman!" (56). The image, of course, is perfectly apt. It completes the earlier one at the beginning of Part Two in which the sun is "filling the hills" and establishes the essential correspondence or interrelation between the human and natural spheres. The man and the priestess are performing only what the sun and the earth have performed and are performing. But through this synecdochical expression of it, Lawrence establishes the centrality and essentialness of the phallic in men's and women's lives: It is their nature within nature. What is important is that Lawrence has secured his meaning primarily through the imagery. To test this statement, one has only to ask if, without the images, there is very much, if any, meaning at all.

It is easy to fault Lawrence for allowing the man to say, "I am risen!" (57). And though the phallic pun, fortunate or unfortunate for the story, has to be deliberate, the punning upon the solar conceit is probably even more so, as the next sentence suggests: "Magnificent, blazing indomitable in the depths of his loins, his own sun dawned, and sent its fire running along his limbs, so that his face shone unconsciously."[4] What his sun penetrates changes, in the next passage, from rock to rose: "It was the deep, interfolded warmth, warmth living and penetrable, the woman, the heart of the rose!" And here is a surprising and effective variation of the expected: not the vagina, but the woman, is the rose. For Lawrence is not describing the physical fact of entry, but a greater, more comprehensive connection. If the woman, then, is the heart of the rose, what is the rose? It is space, the cosmos, all the great natural world including the earth and everything in it:

> But the man looked at the vivid stars before dawn, as they rained down to the sea, and the dog-star green towards the sea's rim. And he thought: How plastic it is, how full of curves and folds like an invisible rose of dark-petalled openness, that shows where dew touches its darkness! How full it is, and great beyond all gods. How it leans around me, and I am part of it, the great rose of space. I am like a grain of its perfume, and the woman is a grain of its beauty. Now the world is one flower of many-petalled darknesses, and I am in its perfume as in a touch. (208)

Several things compel attention (and admiration) here. First, the rose is the perfect figure for the organic oneness that is described. It is both ordinary and lovely. The "folds" of the rose is an image that embraces three immediately previous ones: river, rock, and woman ("interfolded warmth"), each linked by a form of the word. "Folds" conveys the sense of the interrelatedness of all that comprises the natural world, organic and inorganic. The stars "raining," moreover, is another instance of Lawrence's strategy of enfolding one image in another in order to carry the meaning of their organic relationship. This passage, its parts considered together, is the point toward which all the imagery has been converging. The touch that

---

4. Julian Moynahan too precipitately dismisses the story because of the sexual pun: "'The Man Who Died' is a near-success until the baroque conceit of 'I am risen!' destroys the suspension of disbelief required for Lawrence's bold attempt to merge his own and the Christian myths of bodily resurrection" (*The Deed of Life: The Novels and Tales of D. H. Lawrence*, 178). For one thing, the conceit being so peculiarly Lawrencian, it would seem to further the suspension; for another, it is so organically tied in with several developments of the imagery as to make it seem merely another—however striking—part of the fabric.

has brought the man wholeness, integration, that has brought the woman to the completion of her quest ("I am full of the risen Osiris!" [58]), becomes a grain of experience in the "great rose of space," a marvelously integrative trope that itself emblematizes the organic relation among things.

In the denouement—"The spring was fulfilled, a contact was established, the man and the woman were fulfilled of one another, and departure was in the air" (59)—Lawrence does not let the imagery simply wind down. Less dramatically perhaps, but still vitally, the description carries on the story's central theme of connection through a blending of images from different natural categories. For instance, if earlier the sap of a tree had been "blood," now the terms are reversed. The man tells the priestess, pregnant with his child, "Thou art like a tree whose green leaves follow the blossoms, full of sap" (59). As the man rows away, laughing to himself at having escaped his would-be captors, he thinks, "[I have] put my touch forever upon the choice woman of this day, and I carry her perfume in my flesh like essence of roses" (61). Touch, woman, flesh, roses—these are four of the key terms of the story. "Perfume" synesthetically blends the man, the woman, the human, and the natural worlds. A few brief paragraphs earlier, the man has evoked a fifth key term in telling the woman he would not be gone forever: "The suns come back in their seasons. And I shall come again" (60). At the very end, considering how "dear" the woman is to him "in the middle of my being," he thinks, "But the gold and flowing serpent is coiling up again, to sleep at the root of my tree" (61). The serpent, of course, is another of Lawrence's favorite symbols, and the tree is a seventh in the story itself. I take this last statement to mean that the man will retire, for a season, into the integrity of his "isolate self"; the serpent is to guard the tree of his life, sleeping at this root where the tree imbibes its strength from the earth and perhaps from those dark suns inside it. The man rows toward his destination "with the current" of the sea, the last of the story's important images, the symbol both of "loneliness" and connection. The last two pages, then, are a reprise both of the earlier elements of the story and of those that resonate throughout Lawrence's longer fiction from *Aaron's Rod* on. *Ave atque vale* Lawrence seems to be telling us. It could hardly come after a more pleasing unity. With the man, who has found integration both within and without, Lawrence could well conclude: "So let the boat carry me. Tomorrow is another day."

Aldington, Richard. Introduction to *Aaron's Rod*. New York: Penguin Books, 1976.

————. Introduction to *Kangaroo*. New York: Viking, 1972.

Baker, Paul G. *A Reassessment of D. H. Lawrence's Aaron's Rod*. Ann Arbor: UMI Research Press, 1983.

Brown, Keith. "Welsh Red Indians: D. H. Lawrence and *St. Mawr*." *Essays in Criticism* 32 (1982): 158–79.

Cavitch, David. *D. H. Lawrence and the New World*. New York: Oxford University Press, 1969.

Clark, L. D. *The Dark Night of the Body: D. H. Lawrence's "The Plumed Serpent."* Austin: University of Texas Press, 1964.

Cowan, James C. *D. H. Lawrence's American Journey: A Study in Literature and Myth*. Cleveland: Press of Case Western Reserve, 1970.

————. "D. H. Lawrence's Dualism: The Apollonian-Dionysian Polarity and *The Ladybird*." In *Forms of Modern British Fiction*, edited by Alan Warren Friedman. Austin: University of Texas Press, 1966.

————. "The Function of Allusions and Symbols in Lawrence's *The Man Who Died*." *American Imago* 17 (1960): 241–53.

Curtius, E. R. *European Literature and the Middle Ages*. Translated by Willard R. Trask. Princeton: Princeton University Press, 1965.

Cushman, Keith. "The Virgin and the Gipsy and the Lady and the Gamekeeper." In *D. H. Lawrence's Lady*, edited by Michael Squires and Dennis Jackson, 154–69. Athens: University of Georgia Press, 1985.

Davis, Walter R. *A Map of Arcadia*. New Haven: Yale University Press, 1965.

Engle, Monroe. "The Continuity of D. H. Lawrence's Short Novels." *Hudson Review* 11 (1958): 201–10.

Gutierrez, Donald. *Lapsing Out: Embodiments of Death and Rebirth in the Last Writings of D. H. Lawrence*. Rutherford, N. J.: Fairleigh Dickinson University Press, 1980.

Hough, Graham. *The Dark Sun: A Study of D. H. Lawrence*. London: Duckworth, 1957.

Jackson, Dennis. "The 'Old Pagan Vision': Myth and Ritual in *Lady Chatterley's Lover*." *D. H. Lawrence Review* 11 (1978): 260–71.

Jarrett-Kerr, Martin (Father William Tiverton). *D. H. Lawrence and Human Existence*. London: Rockliff, 1951.

Kessler, Jascha. "Descent into Darkness: The Myth of *The Plumed Serpent*." In *A D. H. Lawrence Miscellany*, edited by Harry T. Moore. Carbondale: Southern Illinois University Press, 1959: 239–61.

Lawrence, D. H. *Aaron's Rod*. Edited by Mara Kalnins. Cambridge: Cambridge University Press, 1988.

————. *The Collected Letters of D. H. Lawrence*. Edited by Harry T. Moore. 2 vols. London: Heinemann, 1962.

————. *The Complete Short Stories*. Vol. 2. New York: Penguin, 1978.

————. *The Escaped Cock*. Edited by Gerald M. Lacy. Los Angeles: Black Sparrow Press, 1973.

————. *Four Short Novels*. New York: Penguin, 1976.

————. *John Thomas and Lady Jane*. New York: Viking, 1972.

————. *Kangaroo*. New York: Penguin, 1980.

————. *Lady Chatterley's Lover*. New York: Grove, 1959.

————. *The Letters of D. H. Lawrence*. Edited by James T. Boulton. 4 vols. to date. Cambridge: Cambridge University Press, 1979–.

————. *Phoenix: The Posthumous Papers of D. H. Lawrence*. Edited by Edward D. McDonald. New York: Viking, 1968.

————. *Phoenix II: Uncollected, Unpublished, and Other Prose Works by D. H. Lawrence*. Edited by Warren Roberts and Harry T. Moore. London: Heinemann, 1968.

————. *The Plumed Serpent*. Edited by L. D. Clark. Cambridge: Cambridge University Press, 1987.

————. *Sons and Lovers*. New York: Penguin, 1978.

————. *St. Mawr and Other Stories*. Edited by Brian Finney. Cambridge: Cambridge University Press, 1983.

————. *Studies in Classic American Literature*. New York: Viking, 1964.

————. *The Virgin and the Gipsy*. New York: Alfred A. Knopf, 1930.

————. *Women in Love*. Edited by David Farmer, Lindeth Vasey, and John Worthen. Cambridge: Cambridge University Press, 1987.

Lawrence, Frieda. *The Memoirs and Correspondence*. Edited by E. W. Tedlock, Jr. New York: Knopf, 1964.

Leavis, F. R. *D. H. Lawrence: Novelist*. New York: Knopf, 1956.

LeDoux, Larry V. "Christ and Isis: The Function of the Dying and Reviving God in *The Man Who Died*." *D. H. Lawrence Review* 5 (1972): 132–48.

MacDonald, Robert H. "The Union of Fire and Water: An Examination of the Imagery of *The Man Who Died*." *D. H. Lawrence Review* 10 (1977): 34–51.

Moore, Harry T. *D. H. Lawrence: His Life and Works*. Rev. ed. New York: Twayne, 1964.

Moynahan, Julian. *The Deed of Life: The Novels and Tales of D. H. Lawrence*. Princeton: Princeton University Press, 1963.

Murry, John Middleton. *D. H. Lawrence: Son of Woman*. London: Jonathan Cape, 1954.

Nietzsche, Friedrich. *The Portable Nietzsche*. Translated by Walter Kaufmann. New York: Viking, 1970.

Poe, Edgar Allan. *Collected Writings of Edgar Allan Poe*. Edited by Burton R. Pollin. 2 vols. Boston: Twayne, 1981.

Porter, Katherine Anne. "Quetzalcoatl." In *The Days Before*. New York: Harcourt, Brace, 1952.

Pritchard, R. E. *D. H. Lawrence: Body of Darkness*. Pittsburgh: University of Pittsburgh Press, 1971.

Sagar, Keith. *The Art of D. H. Lawrence*. Cambridge: Cambridge University Press, 1966.

———. *D. H. Lawrence: A Calendar of His Works*. Austin: University of Texas Press, 1979.

———. *D. H. Lawrence: Life into Art*. Athens: University of Georgia Press, 1985.

Schneider, Daniel J. "Psychology and Art in Lawrence's *Kangaroo*." *D. H. Lawrence Review* 14 (1981): 156–71.

Spilka, Mark. *The Love Ethic of D. H. Lawrence*. Bloomington: University of Indiana Press, 1955.

Squires, Michael. *The Creation of Lady Chatterley's Lover*. Baltimore: Johns Hopkins University Press, 1983.

———. "Pastoral Patterns and Pastoral Variants in *Lady Chatterley's Lover*." *ELH* 39 (1972): 129–46.

Tindall, William York. *D. H. Lawrence & Susan His Cow*. New York: Columbia University Press, 1939.

Van Ghent, Dorothy. *The English Novel: Form and Function*. New York: Holt, Rinehart, and Winston, 1953.

Vickery, John B. "*The Plumed Serpent* and the Renewing God." *Journal of Modern Literature* 2 (1971–72): 505–32.

Vivas, Eliseo. *D. H. Lawrence: The Failure and the Triumph of Art*. Bloomington: University of Indiana Press, 1964.

Widmer, Kingsley. "The Pertinence of Modern Pastoral: The Three Versions of *Lady Chatterley's Lover*." *Studies in the Novel* 5 (1972): 298–313.

Wilde, Alan. "The Illusion of *St. Mawr*: Technique and Vision in D. H. Lawrence's Novel." *PMLA* 79 (1964): 164–71.

Worthen, John. *D. H. Lawrence and the Idea of the Novel*. London: Macmillan, 1979.

*I*ndex